SOLVING GARDEN PROBLEMS

VEGETABLES

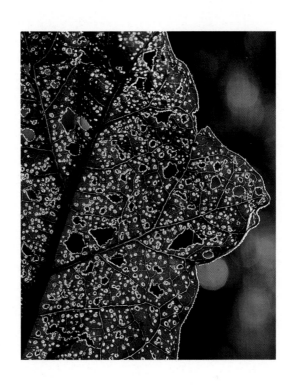

COMPLETE GARDENER'S LIBRARY™

SOLVING GAR
VEGET

DEN PROBLEMS
ABLES

A. Cort Sinnes

NATIONAL HOME GARDENING CLUB

National Home Gardening Club

Minnetonka, Minnesota

Solving Garden Problems—Vegetables

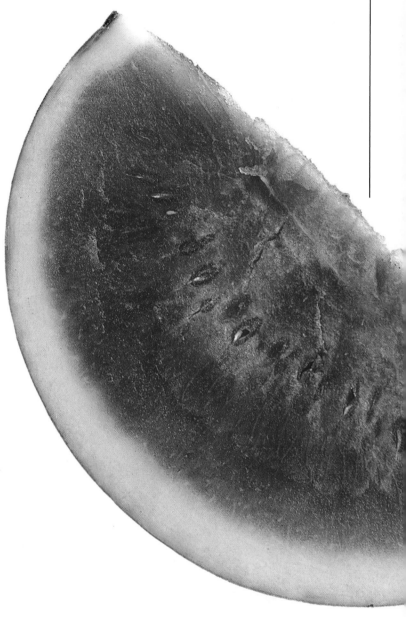

Printed in 2008.

Tom Carpenter
Creative Director

A. Cort Sinnes
Complete Gardener's Library Executive Editor

Julie Cisler
Book Design & Production

Michele Teigen
Book Development Coordinator

Gina Germ
Photo Editor

David Cavagnaro
Principal Photographer

Paul Peterson
Editor

Patricia Langer
Editorial Assistant

Janice Cauley
Copy Editor

5 6 7 / 10 09 08
ISBN 978-1-58159-060-9
© 1999 National Home Gardening Club

National Home Gardening Club
12301 Whitewater Drive
Minnetonka, Minnesota 55343
www.gardeningclub.com

CONTENTS

INVESTING FOR THE BIG PAYOFF

Most home gardening can be seen as a long-term investment in beauty. The blue spruce you plant in your front yard won't come into its own for five years or more; the 'Pink Pearl' rhododendron you plant next to the back door won't really put on a dramatic display of blossoms for three or more years; and even the lawn you start from seed won't really be at its peak until its second season of growth.

When it comes to vegetable gardening, however, it's another story completely: From the beginning of spring to the end of summer we expect vegetable seeds to germinate, mature and produce a proper harvest—all in the space of a few short months. As gardeners we expect a big payoff from a vegetable garden, and anything that gets in the way of that success—whether it's from pests, diseases, animals or lousy weather—causes a big disappointment.

Home gardeners who want the best harvest should remember that the most important phrase in avoiding garden problems is "at the first sign of attack." For all garden problems, whether from animal or insect pests, or from disease, there will be far less damage if you catch it "at the first sign of attack." Plus, what damage there is will be far easier to control. That means you have to be out there in the garden on a daily basis, just poking around, making sure that each plant is getting what it needs and that its path to producing a good harvest isn't being hampered by poor growing conditions, bad bugs or a debilitating disease.

A Healthy Hike

Depending on your schedule, an early-morning walk through

your vegetable garden can start your day on an upbeat note while keeping you informed on the health of your vegetable plants. If a "before your day" walk doesn't fit into your schedule, how about touring it in the evening when the shadows are lengthening and you need a little space and time to unwind? The point is to get out into your garden every day, keeping your eyes open for that all-important "first sign of attack."

In general, insects and diseases "know" to attack the least healthy plants first. The best way to keep your plants in peak condition is to read pages 10 through 21 of this book. If you provide your plants with the right soil, give them the right amount of water and nutrients and choose them with their adaptability to your climate in mind, you'll be surprised at how few problems ever plague your garden.

Also, whenever you have a choice of vegetable varieties, al-

ways favor those that have been bred to be resistant to specific diseases. Plant breeders have made great strides in recent years in producing vegetable varieties that are resistant or tolerant to diseases and pests. Take advantage of the breeders' work—you'll dramatically reduce your pest- and disease-control efforts.

The National Home Gardening Club is here to help our members garden better. And while we don't see ourselves as being an advocate for one type of gardening over another, when it comes to pest- and disease-control, we all must make choices, some of which are considered controversial. To our minds the controversy can be defused by a simple, common-sense approach: Throughout this book the various controls for each problem are listed in order of the most benign to the most extreme, in terms of toxicity and long-term effects on our environment. It's been our collective experience that if your plants are in good shape to begin with, and that if you catch a problem at the first sign of attack, the most benign controls work surprisingly well.

As gardeners, we are, in fact, stewards of this one small slice of the environment—a small piece of paradise, if you will. To that end, we offer the essay on page 30, written by one of this country's most respected garden authorities, Rosalind Creasy, as food for thought for concerned gardeners everywhere.

Good gardening!

A. Cort Sinnes

A. Cort Sinnes

‹ CHAPTER 1 ›

HEALTHY GROWING CONDITIONS, HEALTHY VEGETABLES

66 "Feed the soil and you feed the plant." When you're a vegetable gardener, you can add to this old adage "and the plant will feed you." We grow vegetables to put food and enjoyment on the table. Sure, many of them are beautiful plants too, but *results* are what we want.

The best way to grow the biggest, most flavorful produce is to grow healthy, thriving plants. This means paying attention to the basics: soil conditions, preparation, watering, fertilizing and dealing with pests. The following chapter presents food for thought that you need to deal with before you plant your first vegetable variety of the season.

SOIL PREPARATION
THE ALL-IMPORTANT FIRST STEP

Nothing is more important to a successful, healthy vegetable garden than proper advance soil preparation. Skip this all-important first step and you're simply asking for trouble. Abide by it, and you've taken a huge step in ensuring a trouble-free vegetable harvest.

No matter what type of soil you find in your backyard—from the sandiest sand to the heaviest clay—a liberal addition of organic matter works miracles. The organic matter can be anything from homemade compost to well-rotted leafmold, fine fir bark or peat moss. Almost every area of the country lays claim to some indigenous, inexpensive organic material, readily available in bulk quantities from nurseries and garden supply centers. Some communities even make compost available to local homeowners for free, the material having been made from garden debris and leaves gathered by municipal crews.

The amount of organic matter to add should be equal to the depth that you intend to turn the soil. If you're preparing the soil to plant a lawn, whether it's from seed or sod, the minimum depth you should till is 6 inches; 8 or 12 is that much better. This may contradict some traditional advice, but experience has proven it very successful. If you intend to till the soil to a depth of eight inches, add eight inches of organic material on top of the soil before you till to incorporate it to the full depth. This takes some doing, but it helps develop an extensive, healthy root system, which results in a

Once you've gone through all the work to improve the quality of your garden soil, the last thing you want to do is to compact it by repeatedly walking over it. Notice here how the gardener has used a board to help distribute his weight as he transplants lettuce seedlings.

One of the best things you can do for your vegetable garden is to till in generous quantities of well-composted manure.

Your garden soil's pH plays a surprisingly important role in the successful growing of vegetable crops: Forewarned is forearmed.

hardy, vigorous lawn, able to withstand periods of drought and much more resistant to diseases and pests.

The same holds true for shrub borders, flower beds, ground covers and especially vegetable gardens. Before planting, till vegetable garden beds to a depth of 6 to 8 inches.

Depending on what you are planting and the characteristics of your native soil, you may want to add fertilizer and lime as you incorporate the organic matter. Explain your situation to your extension agent to find out if such additions are necessary.

After tilling the organic matter into the soil, rake the area smooth and plant your plants. Build small dikes around individual plants (roughly the diameter of the root ball), and keep them well watered for the first few weeks after planting. In such superior soil, you'll be amazed at the growth they put on, even in the first year.

There's nothing particularly hard or mysterious about taking a soil sample for testing. The information you learn can make the difference between success and failure with your vegetable garden.

Get a Soil Test

Whether you are planning to put in a lawn, vegetable garden, perennial border, flower garden—any type of garden at all—or if you are having soil-related problems in an established garden, a soil test can solve many mysteries. Taking a test sample and having it analyzed are nei-

ther lengthy nor difficult processes. The information contained in the report enables you to be more accurate in improving the soil for specific plants. And making specific, needed improvements is far superior to the hit-and-miss method of adding fertilizers, lime or soil conditioners in unknown amounts.

Some state universities will test soil free of charge; others perform routine tests for a nominal fee. In the few states where universities do not provide this service, you should contact a private soil-testing laboratory: look in the yellow pages of your telephone book under "Laboratories, testing." If you do not find a listing, call your county agriculture extension agent and ask for a recommendation. Home soil test kits give you basic readings on soil fertilization.

You should collect soil samples three to four months before you intend to plant your garden. This will give you ample time to get the test report back from the laboratory and make the necessary soil improvements before planting.

WATERING

Dewdrops on a leaf: Miniature crystal balls reflect the present surroundings while, perhaps, predicting bountiful future harvests.

General advice on when and how to water a specific site is difficult because there are so many variables: soil type and slope, the plants' specific water requirements, weather conditions—including temperature, humidity, light intensity and wind—and whether the soil is covered with a mulch. These all play a role in determining how much water your plants require.

All of these factors are best known to you, the caretaker of your own garden, so the first word of advice should be to "know your garden": the characteristics of the soil and plants, and how the location of the garden affects your watering. With this knowledge, you will develop an art of watering that transcends the technical advice any book can offer. That said, the following information is a sound general guideline for watering.

either a clay or sandy soil, both of which are notoriously difficult to water properly. This isn't to say that you can't learn to handle a clay or sandy soil successfully, but it's a challenge, involving much trial and error.

Loam, the ideal garden soil, admits nearly all the water that falls on it, holds a large quantity within the fine pores and allows any excess to drain away. A layer of mulch deters excessive

Know Your Soil

First, know the characteristics of the soil being watered. Familiarity with your own soil is the single most important factor influencing your watering practices. If you've improved your soil to the point where it can be called "loam," more than half the watering battle is already won. Plants grown in a good loam soil are far more tolerant of a range of watering practices—whether it's too much or too little—than if they are planted in

Loam is the ultimate soil every gardener strives for. It is ideal in its capacity to allow water to percolate and not cause injury to tender roots, yet it retains enough water to sustain optimum plant growth.

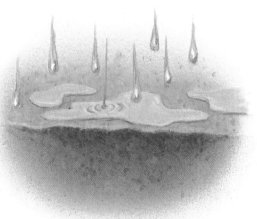

A clay soil, with its minute particles tightly packed together, holds on to water tenaciously—so much so that death by drowning and rot are frequent plant problems in the garden.

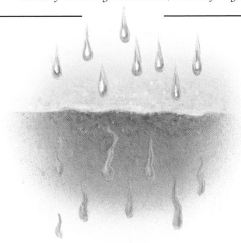

Sand, with its relatively large particles, permits water to pass through so quickly that daily watering is a necessity for most garden plants.

evaporation. With a clay soil, it is harder to establish a proper water-air-plant relationship. Water enters the extremely small soil pores of a clay soil slowly; overwatering causes flooding which, in turn, deprives plant roots of oxygen, causing the waterlogged plant to decline or die. Gardeners who manage clay soil learn to develop a rhythm of what is basically "too much and too little": Alternate periods of wetting and partial drying of the soil, with the drying period allowing air to enter the soil.

Sandy soils provide fast drainage and excellent aeration, but fail in the water-holding department. Generally speaking, the coarser the particles that make up a soil, the less water the soil will hold. Sandy soils (which have the coarsest particles of all) hold only about $1/4$ inch of water per foot of depth. Sandy loams commonly hold about $3/4$ inch of water per foot; fine sandy loams, about $1 1/4$ inches; and silt loams, clay loams and clays, about $2 1/2$ to 3 inches. Although these are rough figures, they clearly show that different soil types demand different watering schedules.

The addition of organic matter to any of the soil types mentioned above will have the effect of equalizing their water requirements. Large amounts of organic matter will increase the water-holding capacity of sandy soils and open up heavier silt loams and clay soils, allowing more air and water to enter.

How Much and When?

While it's hard to give general advice on specific watering prac-

Experienced gardeners know the benefits and drawbacks of each form of irrigation: For all its appeal, overhead watering encourages disease, waste and weeds, while drip irrigation conserves water, limits the spread of disease organisms, and inhibits the growth of weeds by denying them the water they need to germinate.

tices, a couple of time-honored rules can be followed. The first concerns the amount of water to apply at any one time. It is as simple as it is important: Fill the root zone with water and then allow the soil to dry out to a degree before you water again.

If you water too thoroughly and too frequently, there's a good chance you'll cut off the supply of air in the soil by filling all of the air spaces with water. Root growth will stop, and the longer the air is cut off, the greater the root damage. Damaged roots are prime targets for rot-causing microorganisms,

Container-grown vegetables are a very satisfying enterprise, but be prepared to give them the care they need, including regular watering.

There's something satisfying and contemplative about the act of watering a garden.

There are many forms of drip irrigation, all of which are extremely effective and plant-friendly, including this soaker system installed to water peppers.

While they may not be the most efficient means of distributing water in the vegetable garden, there's an undeniable appeal in watching sprinklers make water dance through the air and fall to the ground.

but without moisture, roots will simply not grow there. The result of repeated shallow watering is shallow-rooted plants. If you miss a couple of waterings, a shallow-rooted plant does not have the ability to tap reserves of moisture deeper in the soil. Consequently, the plant cannot survive even brief periods of drought or high temperatures.

To repeat the first rule of watering: When you water, water well and then learn how long it takes for your particular soil to dry out slightly between waterings. Most vegetable crops need about one inch of water per week for optimum growth. Most fruiting plants need ample water when the fruits are forming, but will actually taste better if you hold back on the water a little while the fruit is ripening. You can keep track of the amount of water your vegetable garden receives with an inexpensive plastic rain gauge. If rain doesn't provide enough water regularly—and this will certainly be the case in all parts of the arid West— you will need to irrigate.

General rule number two concerns the frequently asked question: "When is the best time to water?" There are plenty of local prejudices and differing

usually resulting in the plant's death from root rot.

On the other hand, if you water too lightly and frequently, water never has a chance to move very far into the soil. In order to thrive, all plants need moisture, nutrients and air. The soil surrounding a plant's roots may be nutrient-rich and contain plenty of air,

In areas of the country where summer rains are frequent, a rain gauge is an important tool. It allows you to tell how much water has fallen from the sky and when it's necessary to supplement nature's irrigation with the garden hose.

schools of thought on this subject, but common sense may be the best advice of all. You can reduce plant diseases and lose less water to evaporation by watering in the early morning and by not using an overhead watering method. The reasoning behind this is clear: leaves (including blades of grass) that stay damp through the night invite attack by disease-causing organisms. By watering them in the morning hours and at the root level, you give plants a chance to dry off before nightfall and eliminate the conditions in which diseases thrive.

For several generations, the chit-chit-chit-chi-i-i-t of a Rainbird sprinkler signals the sound of summer in the garden.

FERTILIZING

If compost and time are scarce, it's not necessary to amend the entire planting bed with organic material—just the planting holes, dug to about the depth and width of the plant's ultimate root spread.

Garden soils are a combination of organic and mineral components. Two processes make nutrients available for use by plants: **1)** living soil organisms—often referred to as beneficial bacteria—break down and release the nutrients found in the organic matter, and **2)** the natural process of decomposition—the effects of sun, wind, rain and freezing and thawing—make the mineral elements available.

Knowing this, the next logical question is, "Why, if there are nutrients already in the soil, is it necessary to add more in the form of fertilizer?" The answer is a simple one: Although the amount of nutrients in most soils is relatively high in comparison to a plant's requirements, much of this potential supply is unfortunately in a form plants cannot use, or the nutrients are not supplied fast enough to produce satisfactory plant growth. Farmers and gardeners alike turn to fertilizers to make up for this deficiency. Thus, fertilizers play a considerable part in keeping plants in thriving condition—and plants in thriving condition are the least likely to be bothered by pests and diseases.

All fertilizers, whether natural, organic or synthesized, contain some or all of the nutrient elements essential for plant growth. In whatever amounts they are present, these elements are what make a fertilizer a fertilizer.

It's amazing how much compost you can make using nothing more than the "waste" from your kitchen and yard.

Dry forms of fertilizer may be a bit slower and require the presence of moisture for them to work their magic, but they tend to last longer than liquid forms.

Understanding the Label

When it comes time to fertilize, home gardeners may begin to doubt just how simple the process really is—the number of different forms and formulations of today's fertilizer products can be bewildering. And although you wouldn't guess it, the amount of information any gardener needs to know concerning commercially available fertilizers is relatively limited and basic. All fertilizer products have a great deal in common.

The first step is to understand the label. All commercial fertilizers are labeled with the percentages they contain of nitrogen, phosphorus and potassium—the macronutrients. There are many formulations—24-4-8, 5-10-10, 12-6-6, 16-16-16 and so on—but the listings are always in the same order, with nitrogen (N) first, followed by phosphorus (P) and potassium (K) last. Even fertil-

izers that are not complete, that is, those containing only one or two of the macronutrients, are still labeled the same: 0-10-10, 0-20-0, 21-0-0, 0-0-60, for example.

One general rule holds true for all fertilizers: The percentage of nitrogen in the formula dictates the amount of fertilizer to be applied. The reason for this is that too much nitrogen can burn, or even kill, a plant. As is the case with any commercially available garden product, whether it's an insecticide, fungicide or fertilizer, it is imperative that the gardener

Gardeners ask their vegetable plants to produce a lot in a relatively short period of time. A mid-season sidedressing of fertilizer will help speed them on their way to a satisfactory harvest.

The Essential Plant Nutrients

There are more than 100 known chemical elements. Of these, only 16 have definitely been determined to be essential for plant growth, and another one that recent research suggests may be essential. These elements are considered essential because without any one of them, plant growth will not occur, even if the other elements are present in their required amounts.

The box below shows a list of the 16 elements now known to be essential for plant growth. One further element—cobalt—is now thought to be essential for specific groups of plants.

THE SIXTEEN ESSENTIAL NUTRIENTS

The first three elements listed below—carbon, hydrogen, and oxygen—are derived primarily from the atmosphere and water. The other elements are absorbed by plant roots from the surrounding soil. These 13 elements are of primary importance to farmers and gardeners around the world. They are most often supplied by the soil and/or the application of supplemental fertilizers.

Primary Elements:	Macronutrients:	Secondary nutrients:	Micronutrients:	
Carbon (C)	Nitrogen (N)	Calcium (Ca)	Boron (B)	Iron (Fe)
Hydrogen (H)	Phosphorus (P)	Magnesium (Mg)	Chlorine (Cl)	Manganese (Mn)
Oxygen (O)	Potassium (K)	Sulfur (S)	Copper (Cu)	Molybdenum (Mo)
				Zinc (Zn)

read and follow all label directions to the letter.

Not only do fertilizers come in different formulations, they come in many different forms: dry, liquid, slow-release, organic, pelleted and soluble, to name a few. The reason for the great variety of formulations and forms has a lot to do with the personal habits of gardeners. Different liquid, dry or slow-release fertilizers may all have the same percentages of nitrogen, phosphorus and potassium, and even the same micronutrients. But one gardener will prefer the dry fertilizer to mix into a soil mix, while another wants to mix the liquid form in a hose sprayer and feed the entire yard at once. A gardener who specializes in growing vegetables in containers may want to fertilize as few times as possible and use a pelleted, slow-release form.

Root crops, including radishes, need a fairly rich soil, but hold off on fertilizers containing too much nitrogen. Nitrogen promotes vigorous top growth at the expense of the roots, and you want beautiful roots in this case.

Basic Fertilizer Practices

Gardeners who grow vegetables realize they're asking the plants to do a lot in a short period of time, namely germinate, grow to their mature size, flower, set fruit and ripen—all before the first fall frost! In order to keep up with that production schedule, vegetable plants need to have their nutritional needs met on a timely basis.

One of the most convenient ways of making sure the necessary nutrients are available in the soil at all times during the growing season is to apply one of the many slow-release chemical fertilizers. Although they generally cost more, they are worth it. Instead of releasing their nutrients all at once, they dissolve gradually and provide nutrients each time they become soaked with water.

Choose a general-purpose slow-release fertilizer with balanced nutrients: an analysis of 10-10-10 is fairly typical and represents a good choice if your soil is very well-drained and porous. Well-drained soils permit nutrients to filter through them, whereas heavier soils hang onto the nutrients longer. Too much nitrogen in a soil will result in large, leafy, dark green plants at the expense of flower and

fruit. If your soil is on the heavy side, a 5-10-10 formulation is preferable.

Long-Term Benefits

Keep in mind that any chemical fertilizer, slow-release or not, supplies nutrients to the plants without improving the long-term fertility of the soil. Nor does it help improve soil structure. In contrast, the relatively low fertilizer value of organic materials like compost or manure is released slowly, over a long period of time, and they play a very important role in improving the soil's structure and long-term fertility. Experienced vegetable gardeners who know the value of each, often opt for generous annual additions of manure or compost, plus the regular application of a chemical or synthetic fertilizer. Organic materials are best applied after the vegetable garden has been put to bed in the fall, which allows the material to mellow and perform its magic in the soil. Chemical or synthetic formulations, on the other hand, are best applied in the spring, at planting time or just after.

Spraying a liquid fertilizer over plants acts almost immediately, as the nutrients are not only absorbed by the leaves, but by the roots as the excess fertilizer drips off the foliage. "Foliar-feeding" is the ultimate "quick fix" in a hungry vegetable garden.

THE RIGHT PLANT IN THE RIGHT PLACE

Rosemary almost demands neglect: Too much water, fertilizer and benevolent conditions are almost certain to spell disaster with this Mediterranean toughie.

the research. Most nurseries, county extension agencies and garden centers will provide you with a list of the best varieties for your locale.

Choosing Well

Once you select your plant varieties, how you plant them will have a significant effect on their ultimate performance. "Soil preparation" has an unglamorous ring to it, but when done correctly, it can help produce some very glamorous results (see "Soil Preparation—The All-Important First Step" on pages 10-11). At the time you're improving the soil, it may seem to be nothing more than a lot of hard work, but no one step will pay off more handsomely in the long run.

A plant that has to struggle to survive because of difficult soil conditions will grow slowly, lack vigor, be subject to attack from pests and diseases and never quite meet your expectations. One of the most overlooked facts in gardening is that a healthy, vigorous plant will need next to no attention from

Like these lettuce transplants, other vegetable plants are at their most vulnerable when they are young and tender. Slugs and snails are the worst offenders and can wipe out an entire planting overnight. When you transplant vegetable seedlings into the garden, ensure their survival by using one of the protective measures outlined on page 56.

the gardener, while a weak plant will need more or less constant assistance in the form of sprays and assorted tonics.

'Greek Sweet' peppers—classic sun-lovers.

When it comes time to select plants for the garden, most people start with a list of their favorite plants. If you're looking for the least amount of upkeep—and the fewest problems from pests and diseases—this is not the way to go about planting your garden.

Every geographic and climactic region of the country has vegetable varieties well suited to its particular conditions. These regional favorites should always be favored over unproven varieties imported from exotic locations. If selecting the best vegetable varieties sounds like it takes a fair amount of research and effort, it does. But you don't have to be the one to go to the effort or do

RESISTANT VARIETIES

Plant breeders have made great strides in producing vegetable varieties resistant to diseases. With the onset of genetic engineering, home gardeners will undoubtedly see more disease- and even pest-resistant plants in the future. If you've had trouble with diseases on a particular plant in the past, by all means check catalogs, county extension listings and reputable nurseries to see if there is a disease-resistant variety available.

If you are set on planting a specific vegetable for which there are no disease-resistant varieties, the old adage "an ounce of prevention is worth a pound of cure" rings true. For example, once a fungal disease strikes a plant, further damage can be prevented with the application of a fungicide, but the present damage cannot be eradicated.

If you know a particular plant is susceptible to attack from disease, go on the offensive before the disease appears and prevent it from ever becoming a problem. This means applying a fungicide as a preventative before the first symptoms appear.

'Pimiento' peppers, a hardy variety that will resist a host of problems and pests.

VEGETABLES: DISEASE-RESISTANT VARIETIES

Slicing Cucumber Varieties Resistant to Anthracnose

'A & C Hybrid Imp.'
'A & C Hybrid 1810'
'Cherokee #7'
'Dasher II'
'Poinsett'
'Slice-Mor'

Slicing Cucumber Varieties Resistant to Cucumber Mosaic Virus

'A & C Hybrid Imp.'
'A & C Hybrid 1810'
'Cherokee #7'
'Dasher II'
'Medalist'
'Southernsett'

Slicing Cucumber Varieties Resistant to Downy Mildew

'A & C Hybrid Imp.'
'A & C Hybrid 1810'
'Dasher II'
'Poinsett'
'Poinsett 76'

'Setter'
'Slice-Mor'

Slicing Cucumber Varieties Resistant to Powdery Mildew

'A & C Hybrid Imp.'
'A & C Hybrid 1810'
'Dasher II'
'Poinsett'
'Poinsett 76'
'Setter'

Slicing Cucumber Varieties Resistant to Scab

'A & C Hybrid Imp.'
'A & C Hybrid 1810'
'Cherokee #7'
'Dasher II'
'Medalist'
'Poinsett 76'
'Setter'
'Slicemaster'
'Slice-Mor'
'Southernsett'
'Sweet-Slice'

'Tamra' cucumbers.

Onion Varieties Resistant to or Tolerant of Pink Root

'Autumn Spice'
'Beltsville Bunching'
'Brown Beauty'
'Buccaneer'
'Colossal'
'Copper Coast'
'Danvers'
'Early Supreme'
'El Capitan'
'Evergreen White Bunch'
'Fiesta'
'Granada'
'Granex Yellow'
'Henry's Special'
'Majesty'
'Red Commander'
'Rialto'
'Ringer'
'Spanish Main'
'White Granex'
'White Robust'
'Yellow Globe'
'Yellow Grano'

Peppers Resistant to or Tolerant of Tobacco Mosaic Virus

'Ace'
'Allbig'
'Annabelle'
'Argo'
'Beater'
'Bell Boy'
'Big Bertha'
'Burlington'
'Early Canada Bell'
'Early Niagara Giant'
'Early Wonder'
'Emerald Giant'
'Gatorbelle'
'Gypsy'
'Hybelle'
'Lady Bell'
'Liberty Bell'
'Ma Belle'
'Merced'
'Mercury'
'Midway'
'Miss Belle'
'New Ace'
'Pennwonder'
'Pimiento'
'Puerto Rico Perfection'
'Puerto Rico Wonder'
'Resistant Florida Giant'
'Rutgers World Beater'

'Gypsy' peppers.

'Shamrock'
'Skipper'
'Staddon's Select'
'Thick-Walled World Beater'
'Titan'
'Valley Giant'
'Yolo Wonder'

Potato Varieties Tolerant of Common Scab

'Alamo'
'Burbank Russet'
'Cascade'
'Cherokee'
'La Rouge'
'Lemhi'
'Nooksack'
'Norchip'
'Norgold Russet'
'Norland'
'Ona'
'Onaway'
'Ontario'
'Plymouth'
'Pungo'
'Shurchip'
'Sioux'

'Superior' potatoes.

'Dark Red Norland' potatoes.

'Superior'
'Targhee'

Spinach Varieties Resistant to Downy Mildew

'Aden'
'Badger Savoy'
'Basra'
'Bismark'
'Bouquet'
'Califlay'
'Chesapeake'
'Chinook'
'Dixie Market'
'Duet'
'Early Smooth'
'Grandstand'
'High Pack'
'Long Standing Savoy'
'Marathon'
'Melody'
'Nares'
'Salma'
'Savoy Supreme'
'Skookum'
'Vienna'
'Winter Bloomsdale'

'Bouquet' spinach.

Tomatoes Resistant to Fusarium Wilt (F or FF)

'Manalucie'
'Patio'
'Sweet Million'
'Sweet Orange'

Tomatoes Resistant to Nematodes (N)

'Aztec'
'Beefmaster'
'Better Boy'
'Big Beef'
'Burpee's Supersteak'
'California Sun'
'Carnival'
'Celebrity'
'Champion'
'Dona'
'Enchantment'
'First Lady'
'Hawaiian'
'Johnny's 361'
'Lemon Boy'
'Miracle Sweet'
'Monte Carlo'
'Quick Pick'
'Shady Lady'
'Small Fry'
'Spring Giant'
'Sugar Snack'
'Sweet Chelsea'
'Sweet Million'
'Top Sirloin'
'Tropic'
'Ultra Boy'
'Viva Italia'
'Whopper Improved'
'Wonder Boy'

Tomatoes Resistant to Tobacco Mosaic Virus (T)

'Big Beef'
'Carnival'
'Celebrity'
'Champion'
'Dona'
'First Lady'
'Hawaiian'
'Hy-Beef 9904'
'Johnny's 361'
'Miracle Sweet'
'Quick Pick'
'Sugar Snack'
'Sun Gold'
'Super Marzano'
'Sweet Chelsea'
'Sweet Million'
'Sweet Orange'
'Top Sirloin'
'Whopper Improved'

Tomatoes Resistant to Verticillium Wilt (V)

'New Yorker'
'Oregon Spring'

Tomatoes Resistant to Verticillium Wilt (V) and Fusarium Wilt (F or FF)

'Ace'
'Aztec'
'Beefmaster'
'Better Boy'
'Big Beef'
'Big Girl'
'Burpee's Supersteak'
'Cal-Ace'
'California Sun'
'Campbell 1327'
'Carnival'
'Celebrity'
'Champion'
'Dona'
'Early Cascade'

'Big Beef' tomatoes.

'Early Girl'
'Enchantment'
'First Lady'
'Floramerica'
'Gardener'
'Hawaiian'
'Heatwave'
'Heinz 1350'
"Husky" series
'Hy-Beef 9904'
'Italian Gold'
'Jet Star'
'Johnny's 361'
'LaRoma'
'LaRossa'
'Lemon Boy'
'Marglobe Improved'
'Marmande'
'Miracle Sweet'
'Monte Carlo'
"Mountain" series
'New Yorker'
'Oregon Spring'
'Pik-Red'
'Quick Pick'
'Roma'
'Ruby Cluster'
'Shady Lady'
'Small Fry'
'Solar Set'
'Spitfire'
'Spring Giant'
'Sunbeam'
'Super Chief'
'Super Marzano'
'Super Sweet 100'
'Supersonic'
'Sweet Chelsea'
'Top Sirloin'
'Toy Boy'
'Tropic'
'Ultra Boy'
'Veeroma'
'Viva Italia'
'Whopper Improved'
'Wonder Boy'

Watermelon Varieties Resistant to Anthracnose

'Blackstone'
'Calhoun'
'Charleston Gray'
'Crimson Sweet'
'Dixielee'
'Family Fun'
'Graybelle'
'Imperial'
'Madera'
'Smokylee'
'Sweet Favorite Hybrid'
'Verona'
'You Sweet Thing Hybrid'

ANIMALS—THE BIG PESTS

Of all the wonderful birds that visit home gardens, only a handful present much of a problem. Luckily, gardeners can easily protect their crops by covering them with lightweight bird netting, readily available at nurseries and garden centers.

Four-legged pests can be the most destructive threats to our gardens. Moles, gophers, voles and mice may be small in size, but can cause big problems in vegetable gardens. Large pests like deer can devastate a garden. With the expansion of housing and commercial developments, deer habitat is becoming more and more scarce. Many gardeners who never had deer problems before are now likely to confront them sooner or later. To help home gardeners deal with these pests, here is how award-winning garden writer Ros Creasy learned to handle the situation.

Deer Dilemma

One very foggy morning 20 years ago, my husband and I looked out the kitchen window. There on the front lawn, a mere 10 feet away, was a magnificent buck. What a thrill, we thought—a genuine wild animal right here in our cheek-to-jowl suburban neighborhood! It's true that an occasional deer sighting is exciting. But when a family of deer is devouring your every tulip, or you find a buck has snapped a young apple tree midtrunk, it's heartbreaking.

I was once a wide-eyed Bambi lover, but now I've found murder in my heart for these destructive pests. A hundred years ago, Americans viewed deer as a source of meat for the winter. Today, as a nation of urbanites, many view hunting with suspicion. In the meantime, we have exterminated the deer's natural predators, landscaped our yard with millions of their favorite foods and enacted ordinances to protect them. This has resulted in a drastic overpopulation and left many homeowners watching their landscaping nipped to ankle height. In addition, countless deer die a slow death by disease or starvation—in my opinion, a far more cruel way to die than from a predator's attack or hunter's bullet. Ecologists are also alarmed at how deer overbrowsing seriously endangers native plant communities already weakened by humans. In fact, in many botanical circles, deer are considered "jaws with fur."

After years of managing my clients' deer problems as a landscape designer, I've amassed an array of deterrents and barriers to control the damage done by deer. The only completely effective solution I've found is deer fencing, particularly where gardens are surrounded by deer and filled with such irresistible deer yummies as roses, azaleas, vegetables, tulips and fruit trees.

For gardens who are troubled by only an occasional deer, alternatives to fencing are to plant deer-resistant plants, create a yard with large, wide-open expanses of lawn or plant a mass of junipers and other forgiving plants. I've also found that bird-netting can help foil these four-footed foragers.

Fence Me In

As fencing is the most effective way to control deer damage, let's begin by looking at how deer behave and what makes an effective fence.

Deer are prodigious jumpers—it's common for them to jump or leap up to 8 feet. However, given a choice, a deer would rather go under or through a fence than over it. That means the most effective deer fences are at least 8 feet tall and are constructed flush to the ground. (Fawns can squeeze under a barrier that has only 6 inches of clearance. Also, be on the lookout for potential entry holes under the fence made by raccoons and skunks.)

If for some reason a tall fence is not suitable for your garden site, there are other options. Deer are cautious, and they avoid jumping into areas that they can't see. That means you can get by with a shorter fence if you plant a line of taller, bushy, solid evergreens alongside of it. You can also use two parallel 4- or 5-foot-tall fences and then plant shrubs between them.

Electric fences work well and are much less expensive than wooden or chainlink barriers, provided there aren't young children or pets nearby that might accidentally touch the fence. Electric fences are fairly short (4 feet is a good height) and are best constructed with three strings of 14-gauge wire: one strung across the top, one midway to the ground and one along the bottom, 18 inches off the ground. The fences are attached to a power supply and produce a small shock when touched. (The shock startles,

As cute as they are, raccoons can wreak an unbelievable amount of damage in the vegetable garden—all while you're asleep.

but no permanent harm is done.) Smaller (even portable) electric fences can be effective for a small vegetable garden. Deer do not try to jump over these fences but instead put their head or body through, get a shock and learn to avoid the area. Most farm supply stores have materials and information on installing electric fences. And by the way, all fences are enhanced by having a resident snarling dog around.

Other Deer Repellents

Sometimes it's not appropriate or practical to construct a fence. In that case, other mechanical barriers, repellents and/or plants that deer find unpalatable are required. I'm presently involved in a landscaping project with these parameters, and it serves as an opportunity to reexamine the range of control techniques now available.

My clients in Los Altos Hills, California, have a home that is situated on two acres. Their backyard is well fenced, but the front slopes up to the street and was unprotected. It wasn't practical to put a high fence across

DEER DE-FENCE

The minimum height for an effective deer fence is 8 feet. The fence should be flush against the ground, as deer can squeeze through even the smallest space.

Where 8-foot-tall fences aren't practical, an effective alternative is a 4- to 5-foot-tall fence, with closely planted evergreens lining one side. The goal is to create a visual barrier, because deer won't jump into a spot they can't see.

A variation is to construct two 4- to 5-foot-tall parallel fences separated by a row of evergreens. Although this may sound a bit extreme, it actually creates a very effective barrier.

A less expensive—and less conspicuous—solution where kids and pets are not a concern is to use electric fencing. This fence is best constructed using three lines of wire, with the bottom wire 18 inches above the ground. Interestingly, deer don't try to jump these fences, seeking instead to climb between the wires. When they do, the fence generates a mild but effective shock that warns the animals away from further attempts.

One of the most effective, if elaborate, means of controlling deer is to install electric fencing.

the driveway in front, and visiting grandchildren precluded the use of an electric fence. Two does and their offspring also call this lovely area "home."

The aesthetic goal of the landscape design was to plant the hillside with numerous drought-tolerant perennials and ground covers that provide lots of color. The colors chosen were a dramatic combination

As cute as they are, rabbits have healthy appetites and can do big damage in the vegetable garden in a short period of time. Best defense is to enclose the garden with rabbit-proof wire fencing, with the bottom edge buried an inch or two into the soil.

of apricot, burgundy and lavender. I planned to incorporate many plants with burgundy foliage, and a small culinary herb garden was also included.

My first step was to consult the deer-resistant list in *The Sunset Western Garden Book*, the bible of gardeners in the western states. To this list of possible plants I added the names of plants I had used successfully in other deer ares. We planned to plant items that the deer tended to ignore, namely redwoods (*Sequoia sempervirens*), star jasmine (*Trachelospermum jasminoides*), lily-of-the-Nile (*Agapanthus*), bearded iris, daffodils and grape hyacinths. To get a list of "deerproof" plants for your area, contact your local university cooperative extension service. The number is located under the county or state listing in the phone book. In addition, Cornell University has a plant list that is applicable to much of the Northeast. You

can order this by contacting them at (607) 255-2080.

In May of 1996 we began the landscape installation. I was well aware that every deer-resistant plant list contains caveats about not being fool-proof, but it was clear that these deer had never even read the list—over half the plants listed were munched! Fortunately, we had covered many plants (those I thought might be the most delectable) with black plastic bird netting. Thus protected, these plants were fine. However, the uncovered Japanese anemones, coral bells (*Heuchera sanguinea*), rockroses (*Cistus* spp.), potato vine (*Solanum jasminoides*), hop bush (*Dodonaea viscosa*), cape plumbago (*Plumbago auriculata*), yarrow (*Achillea*), Serbian bellflower (*Campanula poschararskyana*), Centranthus ruber, sea lavender (*Limonium*), sedum 'Autumn Joy', yellow lantana (*Lantana montevidensis*), penstemons, gaura (*Gaura lindheimeri*), butterfly bush (*Buddleia davidii*), dwarf lion's tail (*Leonotis leonurus*) and even the new plants of star jasmine were chewed also, most to the ground. The deer seemed especially partial to the plants with burgundy foliage.

Within a week after planting, we sprayed the most common commercial repellent, Hinder, on the plants we thought were most at risk. For a few weeks the deer moved on to the old agapanthus we had divided and the old planting of star jasmine. In the meantime, I attended a Garden Writers Association of America convention and was bombarded with samples of deer repellents by many different purveyors.

Back home, two weeks later, the Hinder seemed to have worn off, and the deer were on a rampage again. For the most damaged plants, we purchased a dozen packages of bird netting and covered as many as we could. Then we decided to test several of the various commercially available deer repellents in separate areas of the garden.

We tested a sack of Bye-Deer, which is made from soaps and herbs and designed to be hung in the plant to be protected; Deer-Off, a spray of putrid eggs and chili peppers; Mole-Med, a castor oil-based liquid designed to repel moles that is said to also deter deer; and small, wicked bottles of predator urine—coyote, to be specific—that was to scare them off.

Rowcovers are extremely effective in protecting vegetable crops from insects—not to mention those other occasional pests, birds.

This was what we found:

1. **The Bye-Deer** seemed to protect the plant it was attached to, but with hundreds of plants on the property, this wasn't a practical solution.

2. **The Deer-Off** worked, as did the Hinder, but again, only for a few weeks. And as we were trying to protect plants over a half acre of garden, it was really tedious to haul watering cans or hoses around to the new plants.

3. **The Mole-Med** had no measurable impact.

4. **As for the coyote urine,** the deer actually seemed more active in the area where it was placed—we found footprints all over the hill. Maybe it was a coincidence, but we had placed one of the urine dispensers near the new terra-cotta birdbath, and the bath was knocked over and broken around this same time. Maybe the deer were spooked by the scent, but unfortunately, it didn't frighten them enough to make them move to a new territory.

Usually found marauding bird feeders, squirrels can also be maddening pests in the vegetable patch. They have an unusual fondness for tomatoes that are almost ready to be picked. To foil their thefts, diligently wrap tomato plants with wire netting (they'll chew right through plastic); securely anchor the netting to the ground. Alternatively, trap the rascals with squirrel traps and move them.

Results for the Long Run

It's now been nearly a year since we first began this garden. We've installed a new birdbath, and this time it's anchored in cement and the top is glued to the base. So far, so good.

One of the does has now had triplets. Aaarghhh! All that great food, no doubt. There are lots of foot paths through the plantings as well as some trampling. However, the bulk of the plants are okay. Recovering under the bird netting are the penstemons, agapanthus, rockroses, yarrows, gaura and limonium. Still untouched are the tall burgundy pennisetum grasses, shore junipers (*Juniperus conferta*), asparagus ferns, bearded irises, apricot foxgloves (*Digitalis purpurea* 'Apricot'), Japanese maple, Mexican sages (*Salvia leucantha*), narcissus, lavender lantanas, euryops daisies (*Euryops pectinatus*), apricot oleanders (*Nerium oleander*

Woodchucks "chuck" more than wood—they're also fond of the goodies found in home vegetable gardens. To avoid damage from these strong, determined pests, enclose the garden with sturdy wire fencing, with the bottom edge buried or securely anchored to the ground.

'Mrs.Roeding'), the Spanish and English lavenders (*Lavandula stoechas* and *L. angustifolia*) and the little herb garden with sage, oregano, rosemary, fennel and common thyme with woolly thyme (*Thymus pseudolanuginosus*), between the stepping stones.

We will leave the bird netting over the large plantings and hope that as the plants mature they will become more fibrous and less tasty. If not, at least they won't get uprooted as easily. Come summer we will replant the successful beds of ageratum and fibrous begonias near the house, because the deer left

those alone. We'll also move the Japanese anemones, surviving coral bells and ivy geraniums to the back garden and replace them with junipers.

What remains is still a beautiful, if somewhat stressed, hillside garden. There are lots of new birds visiting the birdbath, and the hummingbirds enjoy the sages and penstemon flowers sticking up out of the netting. And we've all gotten used to the rather unobtrusive bird netting and are resigned that we won't be able to have all the types of plants we wanted.

What will the future bring besides more deer? Probably a few more heartbreaks. I'm sure we will lose a few more types of plants and suffer more trampling. In the future, I hope to report back on this garden's evolution. It will be interesting to see how this little struggle between man and beast will play itself out over the years. It's a bit of a microcosm of a growing American phenomenon—wildlife and people finding ways to coexist.

When their population gets out of control, chipmunks may present a problem in the vegetable garden. Because they are so wily, about the only way to control them is with special chipmunk traps, available at hardware stores and large garden centers.

When it comes to raising the blood pressure of avid gardeners, moles are right up there with gophers.

Other Pests:

Gophers and Moles

Gophers and moles present a real problem to gardeners in many areas of the country. How can you tell whether it's a gopher or mole causing the damage? A gopher eats roots, including bulbs, tubers, roots of trees, vines and shrubs and occasionally (and most shocking of all to the gardener), whole plants. Gophers tunnel from 6 to 12 inches under the soil and push the excavated dirt out to the surface, leaving small mounds of fine-particled earth. The mounds are not completely symmetrical.

The mole is considered insectivorous, eating larvae and worms, and occasionally tulip bulbs. The mole burrows so close to the soil surface that you can plainly see his route. In the tunnel-making process, moles break off tender root systems, snap stems and uproot seedlings. Molehills are symmetrical, and look like small volcanoes. Unlike the gopher's pulverized soil, the soil that makes up a molehill is in small, compact plugs.

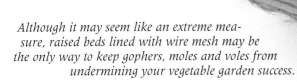

Although it may seem like an extreme measure, raised beds lined with wire mesh may be the only way to keep gophers, moles and voles from undermining your vegetable garden success.

Squirrels, rabbits, birds and other hungry members of the animal kingdom are quick to attack succulent young plants like lettuce seedlings. A simple row wire cover is often enough to foil their best attempts in devouring your crop.

Or you may plant rows of the so-called "gopher plant," (*Euphorbia lathyris*) around the perimeter of your garden or planting bed. The roots and stems of the gopher plant contain a caustic poison that may, or may not (depending on who you talk to), repel furry subterranean invaders. And finally, there is the organized and studied placement of wooden windmills called "Klippety-Klops" that send vibrations down into the soil and reportedly scare moles and gophers away.

All of these measures would begin to take on a comical quality if the damage done by gophers and moles wasn't so infuriating to gardeners, particularly when the creatures seem to outsmart the most diligent efforts to get rid of them.

"Last Straw Controls" include two of the more direct and unquestionably effective methods.

Commercially poison grains are occasionally effective but can threaten wildlife and pets. There are also gas bombs that you light and stick into the hole.

Throughout gardening history, many tried-and-not-so-true mole and gopher remedies have surfaced. For instance, there are those who tried putting a garden hose into one of the runways in an attempt to flood them out: this is of dubious value at best, and at worst, an incredible waste of water. Others have tried attaching a garden hose to the tail pipe of an operating car, trying to gas the devils out with carbon dioxide—which is not only dangerous (and definitely not recommended), but a classic case of the cure being more trouble than the ailment. There are a number of commercially available traps, some of which claim high success rates (if you try these, follow the manufacturer's directions carefully).

Few animals are more frustrating to gardeners than a determined gopher.

If you construct raised beds for your vegetable garden, line them with soil-burrowing, rodent-proof wire mesh before filling them with soil. This sure-fire measure practically ensures a successful harvest.

One is to wait silently for hours over a new tunnel or hill for the creature to stick its unsuspecting head out, then whack it with a shovel or let go with a blast from a shotgun. Local ordinances rarely allow the use of a gun within city limits, but more than one country gopher has met his reward this way.

Prevention Is the Cure

More practically, there seems to be only one surefire, albeit limited method to control gophers and moles—and it falls into the "preventive measures" category. If you decide to build raised beds (garden beds surrounded by landscape timbers, or the like, and filled with excellent topsoil) you can avoid all gopher and mole attacks by lining the bed with ¹/₂-inch mesh wire before you fill it with soil. This is a particularly good idea for protecting expensive spring-flowering bulbs. For individual plants, shrubs, prized specimens and the like, you can avoid damage using the same technique: line the planting hole with the same ¹/₂-inch mesh wire.

Field Mice and Voles

These varmints are usually less of a problem in most vegetable gardens. When present, they may be as hard to eradicate as gophers and moles—in whose abandoned tunnels they often live—but their damage is easier to prevent. Be advised, however, their metabolism is such that they will eat their weight in food every day, which can mean a lot of destruction in a short period of time. Instead of attacking plants underground, field mice (and occasionally rabbits and porcupines) attack the above-ground portion of plants.

While there are several kinds of traps available, perhaps the easiest way to avoid damage from field mice is to cover susceptible plants with a floating row cover (see page 145) or with wire mesh small enough to exclude these pests. Poison grain or pelleted baits are also available, although caution should be used with these if there are pets or young children in the household. And speaking of pets, an aggressive cat can go a long way in eradicating field mice from any garden.

Voles, those little-known garden pests, can hold their own with their cousins, gophers and moles, in the gardening-pest department.

A BALANCED APPROACH

By Rosalind Creasy

In the following essay, which won a professional garden writers' award, author Rosalind Creasy explores some fundamental questions about our relationship to nature. When we put in our vegetable gardens, we alter the course of nature to a degree. We want our gardens to thrive, often to the exclusion of other plants and wildlife.

However, when we think through the process of gardening and the effects our efforts have on our corner of the world, we can reach a new level of understanding and partnership with natural forces. Once we see ourselves as partners, not adversaries, to nature, gardening really becomes easier. We don't have to break out the nuclear arsenal for every problem. Adjusting our ways to the ones that have worked through the ages makes a lot of sense in our vegetable gardens, says Ros. See if her experience can make your gardening partnership with nature a more balanced one too.

Author and garden expert, Rosalind Creasy, in her wonderful California garden.

Over the past 30 years, I've evolved into what most people would call a fanatical gardener. Every inch of my Los Altos, California, yard is planted with some form of flower, vegetable or tree, and I change most of the planting plan twice a year. I get both pleasure and my livelihood from my garden, using it as a source for my photography and writing, and as a test plot for my business as a landscape designer. My entire professional life somehow grows out of this patch of ground, and I work on it constantly.

That said, you might be surprised to find that I am not outraged when I find aphids sucking happily on my ivy. I don't feel alarmed when I see larvae and caterpillars munching their way through a few of my flowers. I almost never spray my garden for insects or disease, even with so-called natural products such as pyrethrums, rotenone or nicotine. My garden is still beautiful, filled with healthy plants that fight off disease, and it's crawling with insects, both beneficial ones and pests. The secret? My garden is in balance.

As I've learned more about gardening, I've changed my approach to pests. When I began, I used chemicals to control them. By the early 1970s I had become heavily involved in environmental issues, and using heavy-duty chemicals in the garden ran counter to all I was learning. In response, I started to use pesticides that were "natural" rather than man-made.

Today, I've moved beyond even that. These days I want my garden to be as close to a

One of the first to recognize the beauty of vegetable plants, Ros Creasy was an early proponent of "edible landscapes," going so far as to plant her front yard with edible plants.

Ros Creasy's standard suburban-sized lot supports an amazing collection of vegetables and herbs, including her favorite variety of corn, 'Silver Queen'.

natural ecosystem as I can manage—a garden where the inhabitants work together to solve their own problems. I am an organic gardener, and then some. My ideal is not to interfere at all with the natural system. Realistically, I'll never reach that. Instead, when I make choices about how I will tend my garden, I base my decision on how much damage any particular act causes to my ecosystem. I've also discovered that I generally don't need any pesticides—natural or man-made—when my garden is brimming with beneficial birds and insects that control the insect pests that would harm my plants.

I've also come to understand that the occasional gnawed leaf or slightly imperfect fruit is the modest price I pay for gardening gently on the earth.

The Holistic Garden

My first experience with a garden whose insect world was out of balance came in 1967. We had just purchased our present house, and the previous owner gave me the card of a monthly pesticide spraying service she had been using. I hesitated at first, but she assured me that the service was safe and that all of the neighbors used it too.

I continued the service, but after watching the pesticide fog settle over our yard a few times, it troubled me to think my children would be

running around in all those chemicals. I canceled the service, but the people there warned me that I didn't know what I was getting into.

Sure enough! Soon my porch floor was sticky with aphids that

One of the most effective methods of controlling damage from striped and spotted cucumber beetles is by using "floating" rowcovers (see page 145).

By adopting a "balanced approach" for pest control, your garden will be visited by such natural beauties as this swallowtail butterfly.

If there's an adult in the household who loves to garden, kids will follow in their footsteps with little or no encouragement.

dripped from the ivy. My bent-grass lawn (which should never have been planted in my arid climate) was a mass of patchy fungus problems. Besides that, whiteflies had moved in on the camellias, and spider mites were everywhere.

Luckily, I met an entomologist in the neighborhood and mentioned my problem. Her immediate response was, "You have a classic case of resurgence, or what we call pest flare-back." She told me that I could, with time, restore some sort of natural balance but that I would need to compensate for the fact that all my neighbors continued to spray. She suggested I start my counter-attack by luring beneficial insects into my yard with plants that provided them with nectar and pollen.

My entomologist friend explained to me that no matter what type you use, pesticides never kill every insect in an area, leaving some insects to reproduce. As a general rule, those insects that consume or suck sap from plants can reproduce very quickly, leaving gardeners to face a fast population explosion if there are no natural enemies around. On the other hand, predatory and parasitic insects (the good guys) reproduce slowly. Many of them also need access to pollen and nectar (usually in short supply in the average yard) at some stage of their life cycle.

That conversation provided my first clue to understanding that a balanced garden, in terms of insects, is a healthy garden.

While my friend pointed me in the right direction, I still had a lot to learn. In fact, my first decade of stewardship of the garden was a period of significant stumbling around. In the short run I was able to cut my pesticide use because I was maintaining a landscape filled with lawn, vines, shrubs and trees—a much simpler proposition than true gardening. I overseeded the disease-prone bentgrass with tough fescue and replaced the spider mite-infested azaleas. That helped, but I still felt compelled to spray the aphids on the ivy and put out poison bait for the ever-present snails. For a while a sort of uneasy truce held in my garden. By 1975, however, garden fever had set in with such vengence that I attended college to get my landscape design degree.

I soon planted every vegetable and flower I could find and then the truce was over. My asparagus plants were over-run by asparagus beetles (a pest imported to this country from Europe in 1881); hornworms and bronze mites attacked my

Not all front yards feature a scarecrow, but Ros Creasy's does. Neighbors are surprisingly good-natured about her unusual landscape.

Every inch of space in Creasy's garden is used to the maximum. Collections of container-grown vegetables, herbs and flowers fill places where there is no soil.

were no mockingbirds to be heard in my area either. Presumably, they left because their food sources were no longer around.

I knew that this was one gardening battle I was not going to win. I sadly pulled out most of my vegetable garden. Then I concentrated on repeatedly washing pests off my roses and fruit trees with strong streams of water from a hose while waiting for the return of the insects with the "white hats." It took two years for the number of good insects to approach normal and it was three years before we heard a cricket again.

Discovering Beneficial Insects

In retrospect, the spraying was an eye-opening moment for me. I finally concluded the largest contribution I could make during my lifetime was to learn to garden organically and to share that knowledge with others. I also saw the real power of beneficial insects and it gave me a new dedication. Along the way, I learned a few things that

tomatoes; flea beetles tore through the eggplants; and numerous diseases disfigured the roses. And those snails were still lurking around.

I decided I would fight back, but only by using so-called organic pesticides. The problem is, organic pesticides usually kill both good insects and bad, so once again my garden's natural balance was upset. (At least organic pesticides are quick to degrade, unlike many of the persistent commercial pesticides.) For some time I continued, trying to force my garden to behave on my terms, with better or worse results.

A Silent Spring

In 1981, I witnessed something that helped solidify and reinforce my belief that a natural ecosystem has the best chance of thriving without a lot of intervention on the part of the gardener.

It was during the height of the invasion of the Mediterranean fruit fly (*Ceratitis capitata*), a pest introduced from overseas that had the potential to devastate domestic orchard crops. The

state of California responded by using helicopters to spray our county with malathion, a broad-spectrum pesticide.

What happened next was a terrible disruption of the natural cycle of predator and prey in my garden, as well as across the county. The malathion killed the medfly, but it also killed untold numbers of other garden insects—both good and bad.

Within weeks, the leaves of my vegetables and roses carried a veritable plague of aphids and whiteflies—so many that the plants looked wilted. I started to see all sorts of pest problems that I'd never seen before. There was also an eerie stillness in the night because the songs of the katydids and crickets were missing. Within months, there

To control destructive pests, like this cabbage worm, Ros Creasy encourages the presence of their natural enemies: trichogramma wasps, green lacewings and spine soldier bugs.

Lacewings are one of the "good guys" in the garden. Their larvae are voracious eaters and can go a long way in controlling populations of "bad guys," like aphids, caterpillars, leafhoppers, whiteflies and others.

have helped me nurture a strong garden ecosystem—tips that can help you too.

For instance, I found out that pest insects are the first ones to hatch in spring. Most predatory and parasitic insects don't hatch until there is food available. That's why I no longer spray the aphids on my ivy every spring, even with an organic pesticide, because I know that I would also be killing the beneficial parasitic wasps hidden inside the aphid bodies and be starving the larvae of beneficial young syrphid flies, which feed on aphids.

Further, I now know that some of the most powerful beneficial insects, such as lacewings and syrphid flies, need nectar and pollen when they are larvae. That's why I now plant a feast of flowers in my garden designed just to feed these good guys. I've also found out that big showy flowers like dahlias, tea roses, gladiolus and the like, provide little sustenance for beneficials.

Instead, I line my flower beds with tiny nectar-rich flowers such as alyssum, species marigolds (Tagetes spp.) and zinnias. I also plant herbs all over my garden for their generous flowers and I let vegetables such as broccoli and mâché (a green also known as corn salad) flower as well. These measures are especially important in the spring when the hatching beneficials need the nectar most. I

also provide a birdbath and bird feeders in my garden, to encourage birds which help control my caterpillars.

In recent years a number of companies have begun selling beneficial insects in containers for release into home gardens. If only I'd had that option after the malathion spraying, I would have ordered lacewings to jump-start my garden. Lacewings are the most effective beneficial insects in terms of eliminating most garden pests. They can be purchased as egg cases and then placed in a garden. A nectar food spray is also available from nurseries to spray in the vicinity of the young larvae; this will

encourage them to stay in your garden and work for you.

The Battle Continues

Of course, relying on natural balance to take care of all your insect problems in a garden has its limitations. Myriad pests from abroad have been brought into this country without their accompanying natural enemies. Japanese beetles, gypsy moths, fire ants and European brown snails run amok in our gardens because they have no natural predators. If you are forced to use a toxic chemical in a garden, it's usually for this type of pest.

Getting out into your vegetable garden on a daily basis is the best way to keep it healthy and pest-free. Problems are easier to deal with when they are caught before they get out of control.

It's not hard to see the intrinsic beauty in this patch of different types of lettuce.

If you must use such a chemical, try to use a selective pesticide that will kill only the problem insect. Using a broad-spectrum pesticide will upset the insect balance in your garden. Always remember to read the label on any garden chemical, and follow the directions carefully.

Sometimes the weather is so extreme that the life cycle of your beneficial insects is disturbed, despite your best efforts. In addition, in our zeal for new, flashy plants for our gardens, we have often bred plants that are so weak that they must be propped up chemically with fertilizers and pesticides in order to have even a fighting chance.

Know Your Limits

Because I understand both what a garden in balance can and can't do, I've made my peace with the fact that I can't grow some plants. Sometimes it's because the pest that attacks the plant has no natural predators; other times, it's because I still haven't perfected the balance that lets predator and prey coexist while still leaving me a reasonable number of fairly healthy plants.

For instance, I can't plant eggplants here (they get flea beetles) nor fuchsias (fuchsia mites have been introduced to this country). The list goes on: no zonal geraniums or petunias

(budworms) and no asparagus (asparagus beetles).

But I've also drawn my own personal line in the sand. I refuse to give up growing tomatoes even though they suffer annually from bronze mites. (I also have a few floribunda roses that I can't live without, even though they do get mildew, a fungal disease.) I help these two favorites out with a monthly sulfur spray to control them. I also use a dormant oil spray on my plum trees to control scale insects. When I absolutely must grow something that my persistent pests adore, I turn to noninvasive methods to repel them, such as using floating rowcovers, a fabric barrier that physically keeps the insects from my crops.

Creating a Balance

I'm learning more every day about the careful balance between predator and prey in a healthy garden. For instance, I used to have a terrible problem with thrips. Nothing I tried worked until I found that the problem was my drip irrigation system. The soil wasn't staying moist enough to encourage a soil-dwelling predator that feeds on the pest. I now keep the soil around my sweet peas and my roses moist and my plants are doing fine.

We don't know all the answers yet for controlling either pests or disease. I don't know why I can't get my particular

recurring insect problems under control, so it's evident that I'm still missing a few pieces of the puzzle. It may be something as simple as the fact that I still have to spray sometimes for disease and that upsets the balance in my garden.

There is still so much more to learn. For instance, some studies have shown that plants under stress seem more prone to pests. One theory says that stressed plants produce more carbohydrates and this in turn makes them more attractive to pests. The lesson? Healthy, strong, well-adapted plants in a garden may not even catch the pests' eyes. In addition, a cornucopia of new pest- and disease-resistant vegetable and flower varieties is available, giving us more weapons in the battle.

Gardening practices are changing quickly, and for the better. My guess is that soon, few of us will routinely ask, "Which chemical do I use and when do I spray?" Instead we'll say to ourselves, "What's out of balance here and what can I do to restore it?"

Kids and gardening go together naturally.

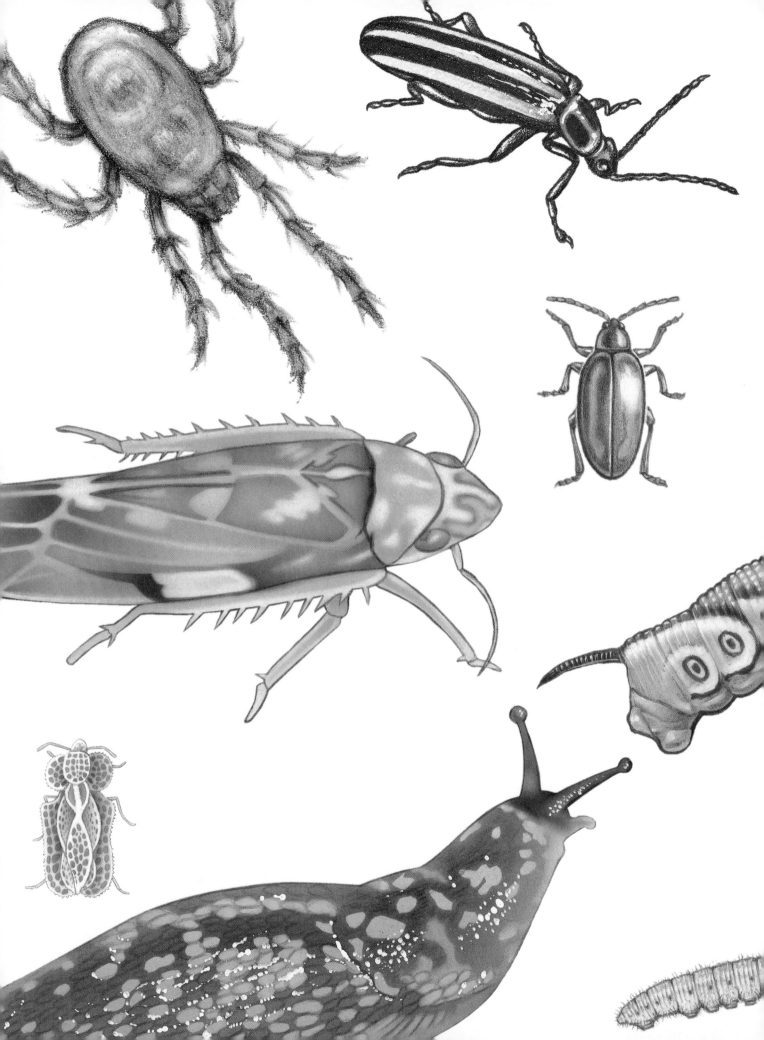

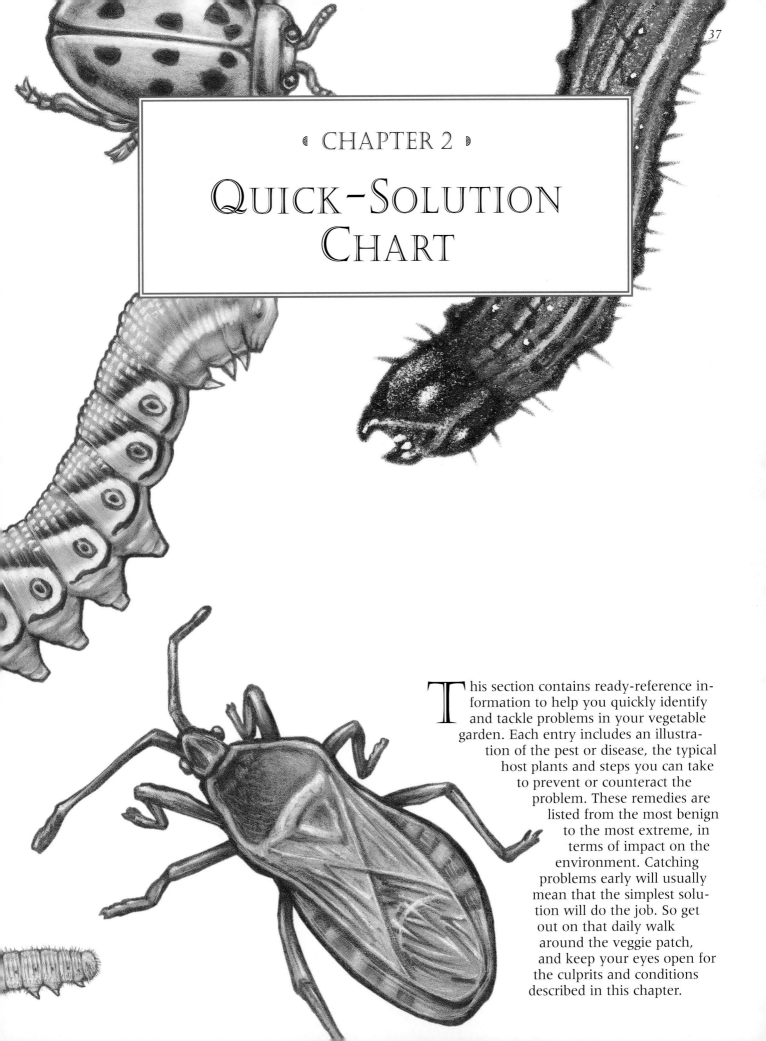

◖ CHAPTER 2 ◗

QUICK–SOLUTION CHART

T his section contains ready-reference information to help you quickly identify and tackle problems in your vegetable garden. Each entry includes an illustration of the pest or disease, the typical host plants and steps you can take to prevent or counteract the problem. These remedies are listed from the most benign to the most extreme, in terms of impact on the environment. Catching problems early will usually mean that the simplest solution will do the job. So get out on that daily walk around the veggie patch, and keep your eyes open for the culprits and conditions described in this chapter.

APHIDS

Symptoms

Clusters of tiny soft-bodied green or brownish insects visible on leaves—especially on new growth and developing buds. Eventually plants become weak, wilted, stunted or discolored. Blooms may become deformed or fall off. A shiny sticky substance, known as "honey-dew" may coat the leaves. Ants are attracted to the honeydew, as is a blackish mold.

Hosts

Asparagus, beet, lettuce, mint, parsley, pea, rosemary, spinach, watermelon and a wide variety of garden plants.

Cure

Start control by encouraging natural aphid enemies, such as ladybugs, lacewings, syrphid flies, soldier beetles and parasitic wasps (see pages 148-149); or by planting small-flowered nectar plants, such as yarrow, dill and Queen-Anne's-lace. Wash aphid infestations off plants with a strong jet of water. Cradle tender growth in your hand while spraying to prevent damage. If infestation persists, dust the plants with diatomaceous earth (see page 142) or spray plants with insecticidal soap or azadirachtin (see page 140). Apply these treatments to both the tops and undersides of leaves. Chemical controls include insecticides containing pyrethrin, diazinon or malathion (see page 147).

ANTHRACNOSE

Symptoms

Small brown specks on pods enlarge to black, circular, sunken spots. Elongated dark reddish brown spots appear on the stems and veins on the undersides of the leaves of bean plants. On tomatoes sunken spots up to $1/2$ inch occur on ripe tomatoes. The centers may darken and form concentric rings. Fruits may rot on the vine.

Hosts

Bean, cucumber, melon, pumpkin, squash, tomato and watermelon.

Cure

Avoid overhead watering. Pick fruit promptly. Stake and mulch plants. Place plants for good circulation. When beans flower apply fungicide containing chlorothalonil (see page 146). Repeat 3 more times at intervals of 7 to 10 days. Continue treatments when wet weather occurs. Remove and destroy diseased plants. Do not plant beans in infected area for 2 to 3 years.

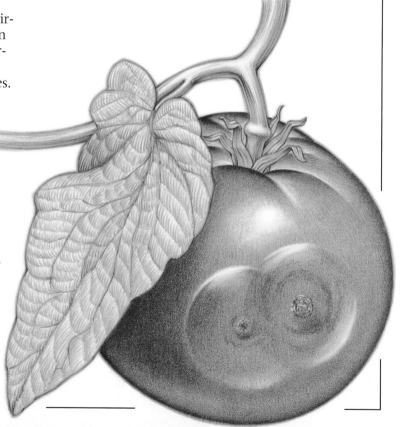

ARMY WORMS

Symptoms

Pale green caterpillars with dark stripes, $^1/_2$ to $1^1/_2$ inch long, eat the tips of leaves. Worms may be light tan to dark brown, with yellow, orange to dark brown stripes.

Hosts

Beet, corn, pea, pepper, spinach and tomato.

Cure

Encourage natural predators such as tiger beetles, trichogramma wasps, soldier bugs and spined soldier bugs. Apply Btk to control worms that bore into corners (see page 141); spray when 10% of ears show silk and repeat 3 to 4 more times at intervals of 3 days. When worms are first seen, spray or dust with an insecticide containing azadirachtin, carbaryl or diazinon (see pages 146-147). Repeat treatment at weekly intervals if plants are infested. Use floating rowcovers (see page 145) to keep worms off plants.

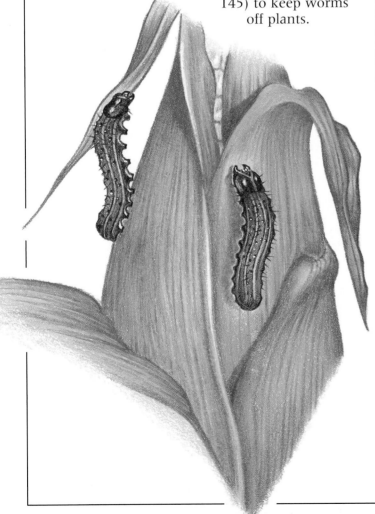

ASPARAGUS BEETLES

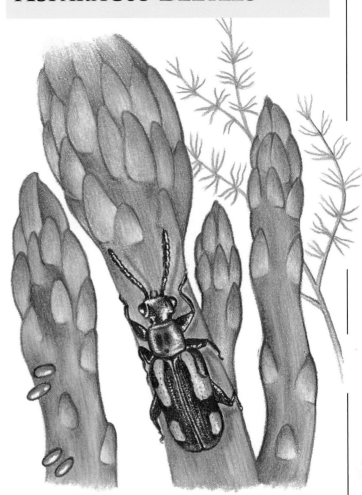

Symptoms

Tips of young asparagus are chewed and scarred. Small $^1/_4$-inch metallic blue or black beetles with yellow markings and a narrow red head feed on tips of the spears, ferns and stems. Shiny black specks are found on the spear tips.

Host

Asparagus.

Cure

Handpick. Wash beetles off spears with a jet of water. Attract beneficial insects, like lady beetles and tiny wasps (see pages 148-149); and plant nectar plants such as yarrow, dill and Queen-Anne's-lace. Clean up garden debris in winter. May apply insecticide containing pyrethrin or rotenone (see page 144) when beetles first appear. Repeat application every 2 to 3 days as long as beetles or grubs are feeding. Treat fern growth in late summer or early fall to prevent adults from overwintering and reinfesting next year's crop.

BACTERIAL BLACK ROT

Symptoms

Young plants turn yellow, then brown and then die. Older plants' leaf edges turn yellow, then progress into the leaf in a V-shape. Older leaves wilt and drop. Veins running from infected leaf edges to the center stem are black.

Host

Cabbage family.

Cure

Choose seed that is certified disease-free. No chemical controls for black rot. Discard infected plants. Place plants far enough apart to allow adequate air circulation. Avoid overhead irrigation. Rotate crops.

BACTERIAL RING ROT

Symptoms

Shoot tips (potato) are stunted and form rosettes. Leaves turn yellow, then brown between veins. Leaf edges curl upward and stems may wilt. Only a few stems may show symptoms. Tubers when cut near stem end reveal a yellow to light brown ring of decay.

Host

Potato.

Cure

At first sign of disease discard all infected plants and tubers. Plant only certified seed plants; if you cut them, disinfect knife in between cuts with rubbing alcohol. Disinfect storage bins with household bleach, rinsing and drying afterward. Wash storage bags in hot water.

BACTERIAL SPOT

Symptoms

Purplish dark spots up to $1/4$ inch across appear on upper sides of leaves and raised on back of leaves. Older leaves may drop. Dark, raised scab-like spots $1/8$ to $1/4$ inch in diameter appear on green tomatoes. Centers of these spots are slightly sunken.

Hosts

Mustard-family crops, pepper and tomato.

Cure

Avoid overhead watering. Do not work around wet plants. Pull up and dispose of infected plants. Pick and destroy all infected green fruit. At first sign of disease spray with a fungicide containing both maneb and basic copper sulfate (see pages 142 and 147). Repeat at intervals of 7 to 10 days as long as weather is favorable. (Bacteria are most active after heavy rain in temperatures from 75° to 85°F.) Rotate crops.

BACTERIAL WILT

Symptoms

Entire plant or stems may wilt; foliage turns yellow and dies. When infected stems are cut, a milky white sap is produced; a knife touched to the sap and drawn away slowly will produce a fine thread of sap.

Hosts

Cucumber, pumpkin, watermelon, winter squash and other plants.

Cure

Plant resistant cultivars. No cure once infection is present. Remove and destroy all infected plants. Avoid spreading the disease by dipping tools in rubbing alcohol after pruning infected plants. Do not overwater or crowd plants. Control cucumber and flea beetles (see below), which spread the disease.

Use floating rowcovers to exclude insects (see page 145).

BLISTER BEETLES

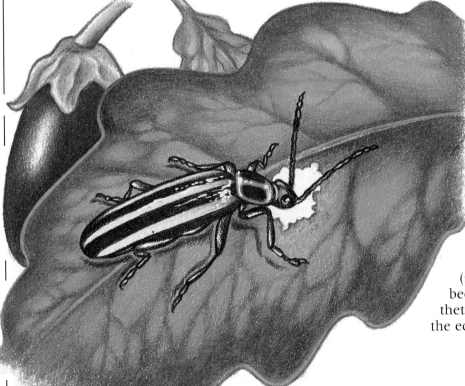

Symptoms

In early summer slender dark beetles about 1 inch long swarm over fruit and leaves.

Hosts

Eggplant, pepper, tomato and watermelon.

Cure

Handpick with gloved hands. Collect and dispose of beetles. Possible to shake beetles from plants and gather with a hand-held vacuum. Floating rowcovers (see page 145) can exclude blister beetles. Cover plants with the synthetic, spunbonded fabrics, and bury the edges of the rowcovers in the soil.

BLOSSOM-END ROT

Symptoms
Bottoms of immature fruit develop dark brown to black spot $1/2$ inch across and larger. Spots may feel leathery and mold may grow on rotted surface.

Hosts
Pepper, tomato and watermelon.

Cure
A condition caused by calcium deficiency. Mulch plants to keep moisture levels even. Avoid overuse of high-nitrogen fertilizers and large quantities of fresh manure. If the soil is salty, leach salts by providing more water at each watering. Drench soil in seaweed solution weekly while fruits are forming. Do not cultivate deeper than 1 inch within a foot of the plant.

CABBAGE LOOPERS

Symptoms
Round or irregular holes appear in leaves. Pale green caterpillars $1^{1}/2$ inches long are eating leaves or florets. When they move their bodies rise up to create a loop.

Hosts
Beet, broccoli, Brussels sprout, cabbage, kale, kohlrabi, lettuce, celery, pea and various other vegetables.

Cure
Handpick. Use rowcovers. Attract birds or insects, such as trichogramma wasps, green lacewings or spine soldier bugs, which eat cabbage loopers (see page 149). Use pheromone traps. Apply Btk, a stomach poison that kills cabbage loopers (see page 141). Use insecticide containing azadirachtin, carbaryl, diazinon, pyrethrin, insecticidal soap or rotenone (see pages 140-147). To destroy pupae, remove plant debris after harvest.

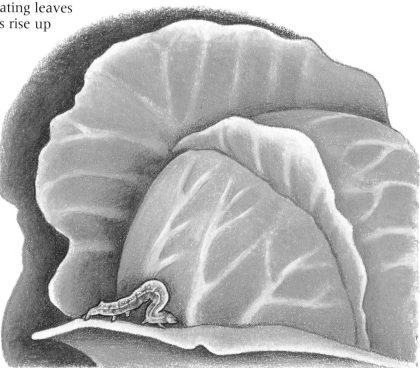

CABBAGE MAGGOTS

Symptoms

Young plants collapse and die. Roots have holes and tunnels. The tunnels are lined with slime and contain small white maggots. Damage is severe during cool, moist weather in spring, early summer and fall.

Hosts

Cabbage, cauliflower, broccoli, radishes, rutabaga and turnips.

Cure

Weed regularly. To prevent egg laying, screen flies from the seed bed by covering it with cheese-cloth or rowcovers (see page 145). Cultivate shallowly to expose maggots to predators, such as birds. Apply beneficial nematodes, which you can purchase from mail-order suppliers (see page 149). Apply diatomaceous earth to the soil (see page 142). To control maggots in next planting, mix a chemical containing diazinon or chlorpyrifos 4 to 6 inches into soil before seeding or transplanting (see page 147).

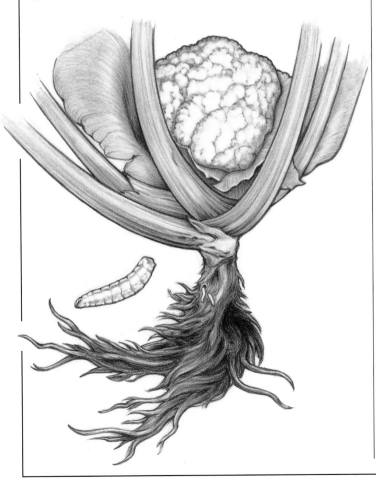

CABBAGE WORMS

Symptoms

Round or irregular holes appear in leaves. Green worms up to $1^1/2$ inches long, with light stripes down their back, may be seen on plant. Masses of green or brown pellets may be found between the leaves.

Hosts

Broccoli, cabbage, cauliflower, kale, radishes, turnips and other brassicas.

Cure

Encourage natural predators such as trichogramma wasps, green lacewings and spine soldier bugs (see page 149). As soon as damage is seen, control with insecticide containing carbaryl, diazinon, pyrethrin, insecticidal soap or rotenone (see pages 143-147). Apply Btk as soon as first white butterflies are noticed (see page 141). Repeat treatment weekly as long as worms are found. Stop 3 days before harvest. To destroy pupae, remove plant debris after harvest.

COLORADO POTATO BEETLES

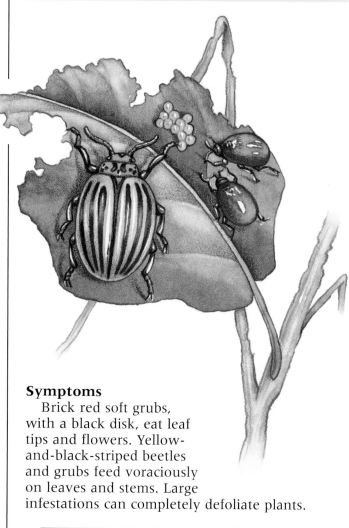

Symptoms

Brick red soft grubs, with a black disk, eat leaf tips and flowers. Yellow-and-black-striped beetles and grubs feed voraciously on leaves and stems. Large infestations can completely defoliate plants.

Hosts

Foliage of potato, tomato, eggplant and related *Solanaceae* plants such as tomatillo and ground cherry.

Cure

Handpick. Crush bright orange egg clusters. Mulch with thick straw and use rowcovers to deter this pest (see page 145). Encourage natural predators such as spined soldier bugs and parasitic nematodes (see page 149). Apply Btsd (see page 141). It kills beetle grubs without harming beneficial insects. Granulated Bt products can be sprinkled into plant leaf cluster. To kill adult beetles and grubs, spray or dust plants with a pyrethrin, rotenone, azadirachtin, diazinon or carbaryl (see pages 146-147). Follow label directions.

CORN EAR WORMS

Symptoms

Striped yellow, brown or green worms eat the kernels at the top of the ear. Worms range from ¹/₄ to 2 inches long. Leaves may be chewed and ragged.

Hosts

Corn.

Cure

Mow weeds or remove nearby weeds that attract these caterpillars. Gently apply fine sand or a drop of mineral oil over each individual ear when the silks begin to show. Grit will work its way into top portion of ear; grubs are unable to chew. To control caterpillars, spray corn silks (while they are still green) with pyrethrin or carbaryl every 2 to 5 days (see pages 146-147). Once the worms are in the ears, insecticides are ineffective. Spray Btk or sprinkle Btk granules into ear tips (see page 141).

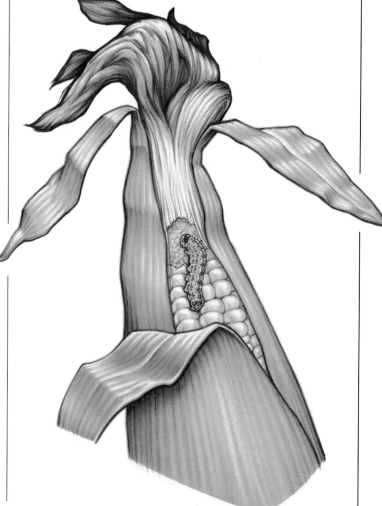

CUCUMBER BEETLES

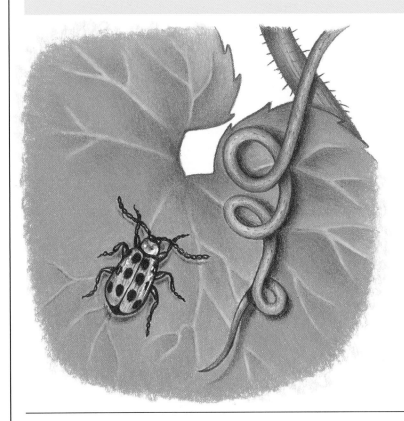

Symptoms
Small yellow-green beetles with black spots or stripes chew holes in leaves, stalks and stems. Plants may die prematurely, or may be stunted.

Hosts
Cucurbits, roots of corn, legumes and many vegetables.

Cure
Natural enemies will help you keep this pest in check (see pages 148-149). Plant resistant varieties (see pages 19-21). Use rowcovers (see page 145). Handpick and destroy beetles. Control infestations by spraying or dusting with carbaryl, or spray with a pyrethrin, rotenone or malathion (see pages 144 and 147). Apply insecticide over the soil surface around the base of plants to kill grubs.

CUTWORMS

Symptoms
Seedlings or recently transplanted vegetables are chewed off near the ground.

Hosts
Asparagus, bean, cabbage, corn, cucumber, lettuce, pea, pepper, tomato and recently transplanted seedlings of all sorts.

Cure
Cutworm collars of paper tubes, cups without bottoms or cans open at both ends are effective. Flood area to force cutworms to the surface, and handpick. Beneficial nematodes may be applied (see page 149). Trichogramma wasps, ground beetles, soldier beetles, parasitoid wasps, rough stinkbugs, tachinid flies and weeding and tilling help (see page 149). Apply diatomaceous earth, baited Bt granules, carbaryl bait or diazinon, or chlorpyrifos (see pages 141-147). Weekly reapplications will probably be necessary since cutworms are difficult to control.

DAMPING OFF

Symptoms
Seedlings may not appear, or may grow 1-2 inches and then wilt and fall over.

Hosts
Almost all vegetable seedling transplants.

Cure
Use clean, sterilized containers and a sterilized, fast-draining soil mix to start seedlings, and water carefully, letting soil dry slightly between waterings. A thin layer of sand or perlite on top of the soil mix will also help avoid the problem. Avoid overfertilizing seedlings. Protect seeds during germination with a fungicide containing captan or thiram. Add a pinch to a packet of seed and shake well to coat seeds. At first sign of damping off stop watering but do not let seedlings dry out completely. If you grow seedlings indoors, avoid damping off by providing as much light and air circulation as possible.

DOWNY MILDEW

Symptoms
Gray, white or purplish fuzz on undersides of leaves, with yellow blotches on top. Severely infected plants will become stunted.

Hosts
A wide variety of vegetables, including beet, broccoli, cabbage, cucumber, grape, kale, lettuce, onion, pea and squash.

Cure
Help avoid the problem by watering plants in the morning, providing wide spacing to promote good air circulation. In fall, clean up and remove all debris from around plants. Rotate crops. Remove weeds from around plants. Prune and destroy all infected foliage. Avoid the problem by planting resistant varieties (see pages 19-21). If problem persists, apply a fungicide containing copper, sulfur, a Bordeaux mixture, maneb or chlorothalonil (see pages 141-147).

EARLY BLIGHT

Symptoms
   First lower leaves develop dark spots. Concentric rings develop in spots to form "bulls eye." Entire leaf may yellow and die. Tubers or fruits develop sunken brown to black spots.

Hosts
   Tomato, potato, eggplant and watermelon.

Cure
   Plant resistant varieties. Throw out infected tubers and plants; do not compost. Clean up debris. Rotate crops. Avoid overhead watering. Space plants for good circulation. Spray plants with fungicide containing chlorothalonil, maneb, fixed copper or fungicidal soap as soon as spotting occurs (see pages 142-147). Repeat every 7 to 10 days.

EUROPEAN CORN BORERS

Symptoms
   Leaves and stalks show small "shot holes."

Hosts
   Bean, beet, celery, corn, pepper and potato.

Cure
   Rotate crops. Handpick and destroy borers. Knock caterpillars off plants with a strong jet of water and destroy. For severe infestations, apply beneficial nematodes, baited Btk granules, rotenone, diazinon granules or carbaryl (see pages 141-149). Help prevent future infestations by removing all plant debris and weeds in the fall.

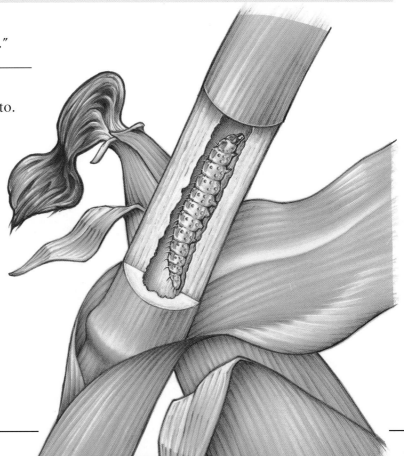

FLEA BEETLES

Symptoms
Leaves riddled with "shot holes" about $^{1}/_{8}$ inch in diameter. Seedlings may dry out and die. You may see small bronze, brown or black beetles.

Hosts
Beet, eggplant, potato, swiss chard, tomato, watermelon and many other vegetables.

Cure
Rotate crops. Clean garden to remove havens for overwintering adults. Gather beetles with hand-held vacuum. Protect seedlings with floating rowcovers (see page 145). Keep garden well irrigated in summer. White sticky traps and diatomaceous earth are helpful (see pages 142 and 145). Parasitic nematodes and tilling are effective (see page 149). Spray insecticidal soap, or spray with insecticide with rotenone, carbaryl or pyrethrins (see pages 143-147). Repeat at weekly intervals as needed.

FUSARIUM WILT

Symptoms
Leaves curl and stems wilt. Leaves yellow and drop prematurely.

Hosts
Asparagus, basil, chard, parsley, rhubarb, rosemary, spinach, sweet potato, tomato, watermelon and a wide variety of other garden plants.

Cure
Rotate crops. Remove and discard infected plants at the first sign of infection. Add agricultural lime to raise soil alkalinity to pH 6.5-7.5. Avoid overwatering. Soil solarization can help (see page 150).
Plant resistant varieties.

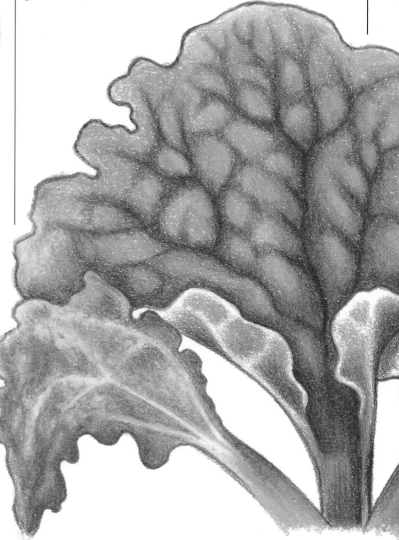

GRASSHOPPERS

Symptoms

Tender seedlings will be the first casualties to grasshoppers. Large holes will appear around the edges of leaves of all types of plants, as grasshoppers continue their feeding.

Hosts

A wide variety of garden plants including basil and swiss chard.

Cure

If infestation is not large, handpick and destroy insects. Attract birds, which eat grasshoppers, by providing water and shrubby nesting places. Plant nectar plants such as dill, yarrow or Queen-Anne's-lace to attract predator insects. Use beneficial nematodes to go after eggs (see page 149). Till the soil in autumn to expose eggs. For severe infestations, spray with an insecticide containing neem, carbaryl, diazinon or malathion (see pages 140-147). Problems with grasshoppers in the future can be avoided with an application of *Nosema locustae* (see page 144), but it works best when applied over a wide area, as opposed to just one yard.

JAPANESE BEETLES

Symptoms

Leaves and flowers skeletonized or chewed in lacy pattern.

Hosts

Asparagus, basil, rhubarb and many garden plants.

Cure

Trap adults in commercial traps hung well downwind of crops. Use floating rowcovers (see page 145). If infestation is not large, handpick and destroy insects. For larger infestations use insecticidal soap or spray with azadirachtin (see pages 140 and 143). As a last resort, spray with insecticide containing pyrethrum, rotenone, carbaryl or malathion (see pages 146-147). To avoid future problems with beetles, apply parasitic nematodes or milky disease spores to soil (see page 149).

LACE BUGS

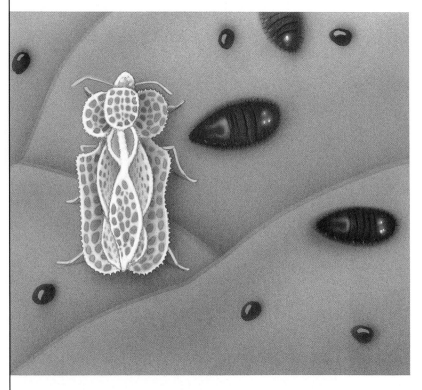

Symptoms

Foliage appears speckled, splotched or striped with bleached-looking spots. Shiny, hard black droplets on the undersides of damaged leaves.

Hosts

Many garden plants.

Cure

Pick off and destroy infested leaves. Start by handpicking and destroying insects, or spray with insecticidal soap (see page 143). Be sure to spray both tops and undersides of leaves. Use white sticky traps (see page 145). If infestation persists, spray with an insecticide containing pyrethrum, malathion, diazinon or carbaryl (see pages 146-147). Avoid future problems by attracting lace bug's natural insect enemies with plantings of alyssum and dill.

LATE BLIGHT

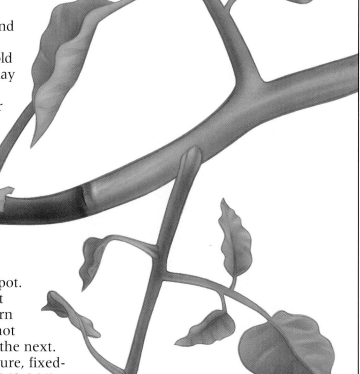

Symptoms

Small, dark, water-soaked spots appear on leaves and stems. They may rapidly enlarge to purplish black lesions, under cool, moist conditions. White or gray mold may appear on the leaf undersides. Fruits or tubers may shrivel and rot. In cool, wet weather, late blight may advance rapidly and ruin an entire field of potatoes or tomatoes in a few days.

Hosts

Tomato and potato.

Cure

Plant certified seed potatoes. Remove and destroy infected leaves of tomato or potato as soon as they show a spot. Improve drainage. Avoid overhead watering. Do not harvest potatoes when soil is wet; wait till plants turn yellow and die naturally to harvest the potato. Do not compost or hold over potato seed from one year to the next. In early spring, spray tomatoes with Bordeaux mixture, fixed-copper fungicidal soap or chlorothalonil (see pages 142-146). Follow label directions. Rotate crops.

LEAFHOPPERS

Symptoms

Plant leaves may be stippled. Severe infestations may cause stunting and leaf drop.

Hosts

Bean, celery, eggplant, potato and many vegetables.

Cure

Use rowcovers (see page 145). Weed area that may harbor leafhopper eggs. Spray insects off plants with a strong spray of water. Use diatomaceous earth (see page 142). Use yellow sticky traps. Natural predators include birds, green lacewings and parasitoid wasps (see page 149). Apply insecticidal soap (see page 143). Spray infested plants with an insecticide containing diazinon, pyrethrin, azadirachtin, rotenone, malathion or carbaryl (see pages 140-147). Cover tops and undersides of leaves. Respray to control insect. Wait 10 days between applications.

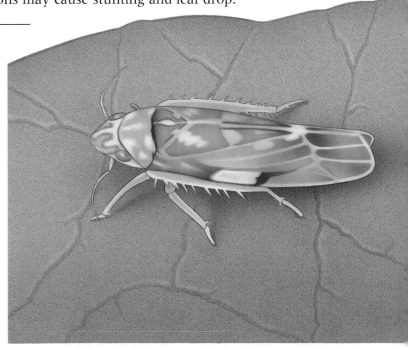

LEAF MINERS

Symptoms

Light tan, winding trails or blotches on or in leaves. Plants may be stunted or killed.

Hosts

A wide variety of garden vegetables.

Cure

Use floating rowcovers (see page 145). Pick and destroy affected leaves. Natural controls include attracting parasitic wasps (see page 149). Use yellow sticky traps. Avoid future damage by treating the soil with beneficial nematodes (see page 149).

LEAF ROLLERS

Symptoms

Leaves rolled into tubes, tied with fine, sticky webbing; when unrolled, leaves contain feeding caterpillars inside.

Hosts

A wide variety of vegetable plants.

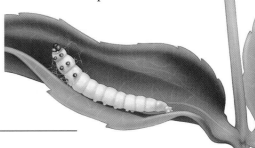

Cure

Use rowcovers (see page 145). Handpick and destroy caterpillar-infested leaves. Dust with Btk (see page 141) on a regular basis and encourage leafroller's natural enemies, such as birds and parasitoid trichogramma wasps and spined soldier bugs. (see page 149). Chemical controls include insecticides containing diazanon or carbaryl (see pages 146-147), but are most effective when applied before the larvae are protected inside the rolled leaves. Avoid the problem in the future with a winter spray of dormant oil (see page 143).

LEAF SPOTS

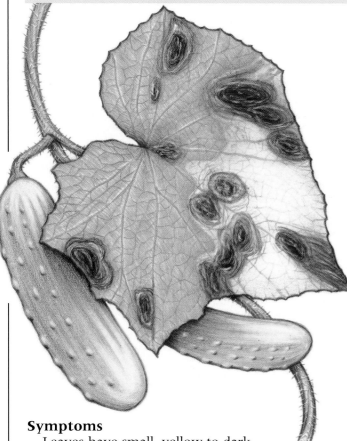

Symptoms
Leaves have small, yellow to dark brown spots with purplish-black sunken areas; grayish-brown dead areas eventually develop in the center of the spot. Leaf tissues around spot may turn yellow. Lesions develop on stems, especially at bases. The entire plant may eventually wilt and die.

Hosts
Many vegetable plants.

Cure
Rotate crops. Clean all debris and weeds from around plants. Remove and destroy leaves as soon as possible. Do not compost. Clean tools with rubbing alcohol after pruning infected plants. If totally infected, remove and destroy plant. Water plants in the morning. Space plants widely to allow good air circulation. Fertilize well throughout the growing season and remove all garden debris regularly. At first sign of disease treat with a fungicide containing chlorothalonil or captan (see page 146). If disease persists, spray weekly with sulfur or a fungicide containing chlorothalonil (see pages 145-146). Dig compost into soil after harvesting crop.

MEXICAN BEAN BEETLES

Symptoms
The tissue between leaf veins is eaten. Copper-colored beetles, each with 16 black spots, about $1/4$ inch long, feed on the undersides of the skeletonized leaves. Stems and pods may be eaten. Orange to yellow soft-bodied grubs about $1/3$ inch long with black-tipped spines on their backs may also be present. Worst damage happens in July and August. Plant may die.

Hosts
Bush bean, cowpea and lima bean.

Cure
Rowcovers (see page 145), sanitation, handpicking, trap crops. Shake these beetles from their roosts onto a cloth and then discard them. After the harvest remove and destroy all plant debris to reduce overwintering spots for adults. Encourage natural enemies such as toads, birds, tachinid flies and parasitoid wasps (see page 149). When the adults first appear apply an insecticide containing azadirachtin, carbaryl, rotenone, pyrethrum, malathion or diazinon (see pages 140-147). Spray the undersides of the leaves, where the insects feed. For larvae use bean beetle parasites or spined soldierbugs.

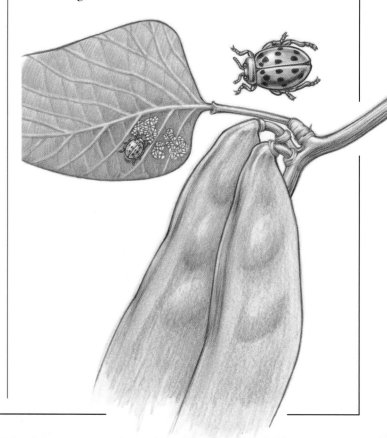

NEMATODES

Symptoms

Damage causes leaves to yellow and become stunted or wilt. Roots look stunted and show lumpy nodules that shelter nematodes and help them siphon off nutrients and water.

Hosts

Corn, lettuce, onion, pepper, potato and tomato.

Cure

Plant resistant varieties; marigolds discourage nematodes. Soil solarization and crop rotation are the most effective treatment (see page 150). Pull and destroy infected plants, including roots. Natural enemies include a soil fungus that can be encouraged by digging in organic matter such as leaf mold. In severe cases use professional soil fumigation. Apply Nematrol or incorporate chitin into the soil, which may also control pests (see page 141).

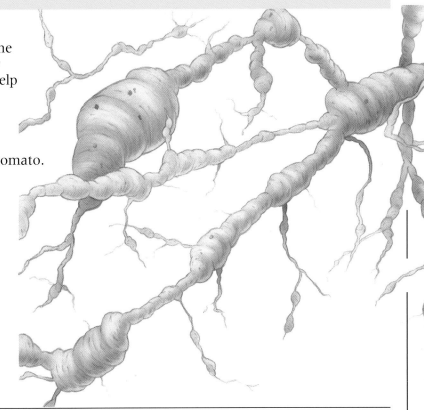

ONION MAGGOTS

Symptoms

Plants grow slowly, turn yellow, wilt and die. Small holes riddle onion stems just below the soil line. Bulbs may rot in storage. White maggots up to $1/3$ inch burrow inside the bulbs.

Hosts

Onion, leek.

Cure

Use rowcovers and apply beneficial nematodes (see pages 145 and 149). Rotate crops. Discard and destroy maggot-infested onions. Remove all debris from garden at the end of the season to reduce overwintering pupae. At planting time treat soil with chemical containing diazinon or chlorpyrifos (see page 147).

PINK ROOT

Symptoms

Plants grow slowly but show no other symptoms. The roots are pinkish brown. Leaves may turn yellow or white and then die.

Hosts

Onion, garlic, shallot, leek and chive.

Cure

Plant resistant varieties. Rotate crops to minimize the disease. Compost plant debris. Pink root fungus can be removed from the soil only by fumigation techniques.

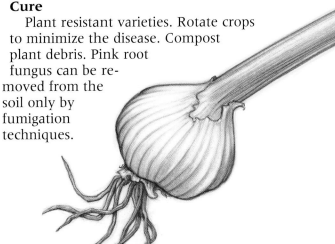

POWDERY MILDEW

Symptoms

Grayish, powdery-white coating appears on leaves, flowers and stems. Plants usually do not die, but infected leaves eventually turn yellow.

Hosts

A variety of vegetables, including bean, cucumber, pea, pumpkin and winter squash.

Cure

Dig up and destroy severely infected plants. To prevent future outbreaks, spray with baking soda. To make baking soda spray, dissolve 1 teaspoon baking soda in 1 quart warm water; add 1 teaspoon insecticidal soap to make the solution stick to the leaves (see page 141). Use at intervals of 10 to 12 days to protect new growth. Spray with fixed copper spray, wettable sulfur spray or a fungicide containing chlorothalonil (see page 146). Clean up and remove plant debris in the fall.

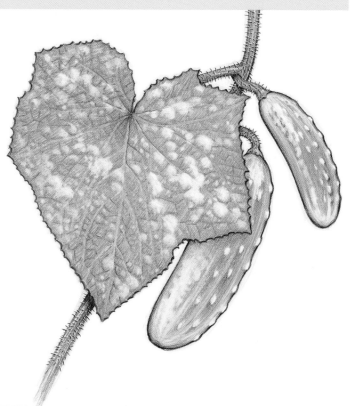

ROOT MAGGOTS

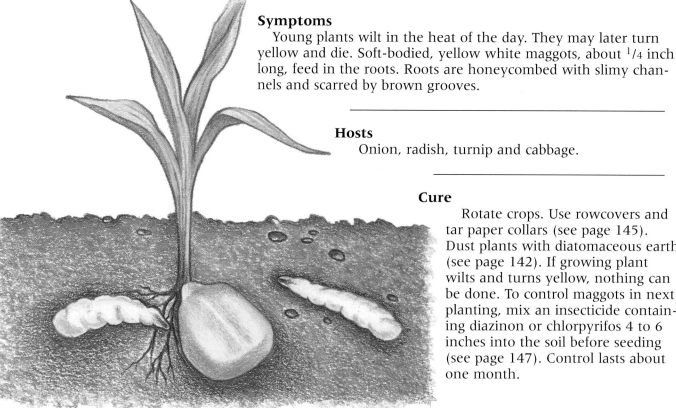

Symptoms

Young plants wilt in the heat of the day. They may later turn yellow and die. Soft-bodied, yellow white maggots, about $1/4$ inch long, feed in the roots. Roots are honeycombed with slimy channels and scarred by brown grooves.

Hosts

Onion, radish, turnip and cabbage.

Cure

Rotate crops. Use rowcovers and tar paper collars (see page 145). Dust plants with diatomaceous earth (see page 142). If growing plant wilts and turns yellow, nothing can be done. To control maggots in next planting, mix an insecticide containing diazinon or chlorpyrifos 4 to 6 inches into the soil before seeding (see page 147). Control lasts about one month.

ROOT ROT

Symptoms

Leaves and stems turn yellow, wilt and die. The lower leaves and stems may be soft and rotted. White fungal strands may grow around the bases of plants.

Hosts

Many vegetable plants, including beet.

Cure

Allow the soil to dry out around the plant between waterings. Remove and destroy infected plants and soil immediately surrounding the roots. Avoid the problem by improving the soil drainage with regular additions of an organic soil amendment, such as compost. Avoid overwatering. If this disease persists, you may have to start new disease-free plants in a different garden location.

RUST

Symptoms

Leaves and stems have red or orange powdery spots and streaks, followed by yellow or dark splotches on tops.

Hosts

Many vegetables, such as asparagus, bean, beet, carrot, corn, onion, spinach and herbs including mint.

Cure

Remove and destroy infected leaves. Spray infected leaves with sulfur, Bordeaux mixture or a fungicide containing chlorothalonil (see page 146). Avoid overhead watering. Water early in the day so plants will dry out before nightfall. Space or thin plants for good air circulation. Avoid splashing water on the foliage. Remove and compost all garden debris in the fall.

SLUGS AND SNAILS

Symptoms

Large holes in leaves and stems; whole plants may be defoliated. Shiny slime trails are on foliage or surrounding soil.

Hosts

Many vegetable plants: asparagus, basil, bean, beet, lettuce, parsley, potato, spinach, summer squash; especially young, tender transplants.

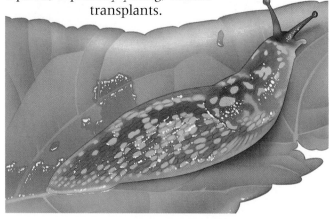

Cure

Handpick and destroy. Put dishes among plants baited with beer. Encircle plants with copper strips (available at nurseries and garden centers, see page 142). Apply diatomaceous earth or wood ashes to the ground around plants (see page 142). Reapply after rains. Sprinkle planting beds with a bait containing iron phosphate, metaldehyde or methiocarb (see pages 144 and 147) but be careful not to get these baits anywhere near fish as they are highly toxic to the fish. Encourage natural enemies of snails and slugs: birds, toads, salamanders and predacious ground beetles. Chickens, geese and ducks are also efficient snail hunters.

SOFT ROT

Symptoms

Water-soaked spots on fruits and vegetables enlarge and become sunken. Sometimes there is a foul odor; plants are yellowed and stunted.

Hosts

Many vegetables.

Cure

There is no cure for this disease. Remove and destroy all plants showing signs of decay. Disinfect tools with bleach. Space plants widely to encourage good air circulation. Plant in well-drained soil, and do not overwater.

SPIDER MITES

Symptoms
Flowers and leaves turn yellow, bronze or speckled. Fine webbing may appear on undersides of leaves. Affected leaves may drop prematurely.

Hosts
Many plants, including asparagus, rosemary and watermelon.

Cure
Avoid the problem by attracting beneficial insects by growing small-flowered nectar plants, such as alyssum and dill. Knock mites off with a strong stream of water. Use diatomaceous earth to dust the whole plant (see page 142). Apply light horticultural oil to smother (see page 143). If infestation persists, spray with insecticidal soap or pyrethrum (see pages 143 and 147). Dust the undersides of the plant's leaves with garden sulfur (see page 145). Introduce ladybugs, lacewings and predatory mites into your garden to help control these pests (see pages 148-149).

SQUASH BUGS

Symptoms
Seedlings show wilting and are slow to develop true leaves. May be puckering of immature leaves. Squash and pumpkin leaves wilt and become black and crisp. Bright green to dark gray or brown flat-backed bugs, about $1/2$ inch long, cluster on the plants.

Hosts
Squash and pumpkin, cucumber, melon and winter squash.

Cure
Plant varieties that are resistant to attack by squash bugs (see pages 19-21). Use floating rowcovers (see page 145). Train plants on trellises. Handpick. Knock off with a strong stream of water. Vacuum up the bugs with a handheld vacuum. Spine soldier bugs provide a natural control. Nymphs and adults can be killed by spraying the undersides of the plant's leaves with an insecticidal soap (see page 143). When bugs first appear, treat the plants and the soil around them with an insecticide containing carbaryl, insecticidal soap or pyrethrin (see pages 143-147). Repeat the treatment every 7 days until the bugs are controlled. Rotenone and malathion are effective (see pages 144 and 147).

SQUASH VINE BORERS

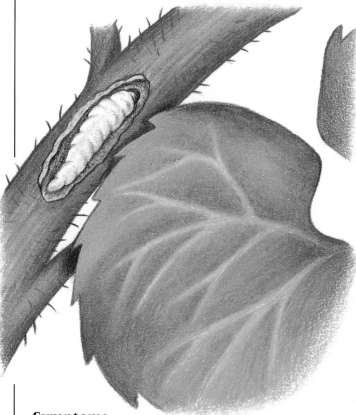

Symptoms

Vines sud-
denly wilt and collapse, even though plants may
be well watered. Bubbly greenish-yellow insect
excrement appear near the holes in the stems.
Wilted plants usually die.

Hosts

Squash and pumpkin and occasionally cucumber and melon.

Cure

Use rowcovers, foil collars around the lower
stem; trichogramma wasps or a trap crop help
control an infestation (see page 149). Handpick.
Dust the base of the plants with rotenone, a
pyrethrum product, malathion or carbaryl, every
7 to 10 days, after vines begin to run (see pages
144-147). Insecticides are useless once the borer
has penetrated the vine. Cut away the infected
vines. You may try to kill the pest by injecting
beneficial nematodes or 3 cc of Btk into stems
with a syringe (see pages 141 and 149). Pull up
all plant debris after harvest, and destroy crop
debris. Till the soil to kill the resting pupae.

THRIPS

Symptoms

White or silver streaks or blotches appear on
leaves. Tips may be distorted. Plants may wilt,
wither, turn brown and die. Bulbs may be distorted
and small. Small, pale, green to white insects are
observed at the base of the leaves.

Hosts

Most vegetables, including bean, cucumber,
melon, onion and tomato.

Cure

Knock thrips off plants with a strong spray of
water. Clear weeds from around the plants. Spray
plants with an insecticidal soap (see page 143).
Encourage beneficial insects by growing the small-
flowered nectar plants such as alyssum and dill.
Apply horticultural oil or azadirachtin to the plants
(see pages 140 and 143). Hang blue or yellow
sticky traps (see page 145). Green lacewings and
predatory mites, sulfur, diatomaceous earth, soap
and oil sprays can also be used to help control an
infestation (see pages 142-149). At first signs of
thrips damage, treat infested plants with insecticide
containing diazinon, pyrethrum, rotenone or
malathion (see pages 144-147). Repeat at weekly
intervals until new
growth is no longer
damaged.

TOBACCO HORNWORMS

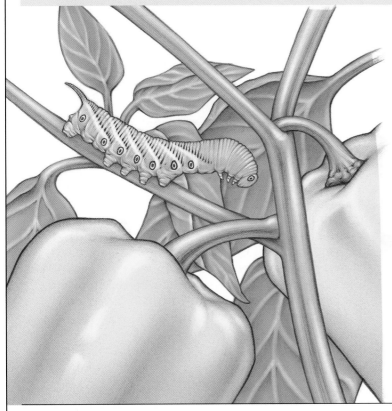

Symptoms
Fat green or brown worms, with white stripes and a red or black "horn" on their rear end, chew on leaves. They can be up to 5 inches long. Black droppings soil the leaves.

Hosts
Tomato, potato, tobacco, pepper or eggplant.

Cure
Handpick. Natural enemies are birds, lacewing larvae and parasitoid wasps (see page 149). Spraying in the early evening with Btk may kill smaller caterpillars (see page 141). Treat the plants with an insecticide containing carbaryl, pyrethrin, rotenone or diazinon (see pages 146-147). Do not destroy worms covered in a white sac; let wasps inside the worms mature, emerge and infest the other hornworms.

TOBACCO MOSAIC VIRUS

Symptoms
Leaves distorted or smaller than normal, mottled with spots of yellow, white or brown. In some cases the foliage develops yellow rings.

Hosts
Eggplant, pepper, potato, tomato and a variety of garden vegetables.

Cure
Plant resistant varieties. Dig up and destroy infected plants. Avoid all contact with tobacco products. Sterilize hands, tools and gloves.

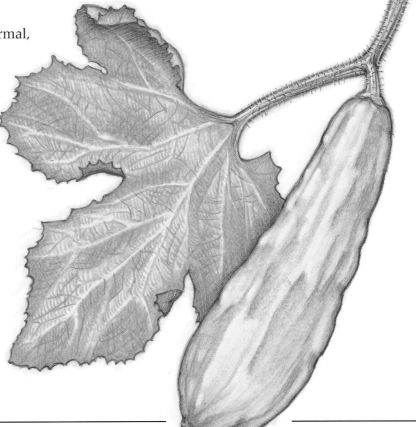

TOMATO GROWTH CRACKS

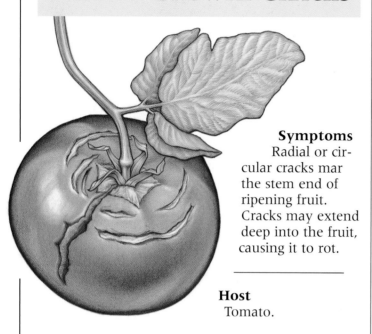

Symptoms
Radial or circular cracks mar the stem end of ripening fruit. Cracks may extend deep into the fruit, causing it to rot.

Host
Tomato.

Cure
Grow varieties that are crack tolerant. Maintain an even soil moisture with regular watering.

VERTICILLIUM WILT

Symptoms
Leaf color usually dull; leaves may yellow and wilt. The plant loses vigor and may die; it may happen quickly or over the course of months.

Hosts
Many vegetables including bean, potato, rhubarb, strawberry and tomato.

Cure
Rotate crops. Plant resistant varieties and reduce nitrogen fertilizer. Avoid overwatering or severe pruning. Space plants widely. Soil solarization can help (see page 150). Use new sterilized soil in containers. There is no chemical control.

TOMATO HORNWORMS

Symptoms
Buds, leaves, flowers and even fruit may be chewed to tatters or eaten entirely.

Hosts
Tomato, pepper and watermelon.

Cure
Handpick. Natural enemies are birds, lacewing larvae and parasitoid wasps (see page 149). Spraying in the early evening with Btk may kill smaller caterpillars (see page 141). Treat the plants with an insecticide containing carbaryl, pyrethrin, rotenone or diazinon (see pages 146-147). Do not destroy worms covered in a white sac; let wasps inside the worms mature, emerge and infest the other hornworms.

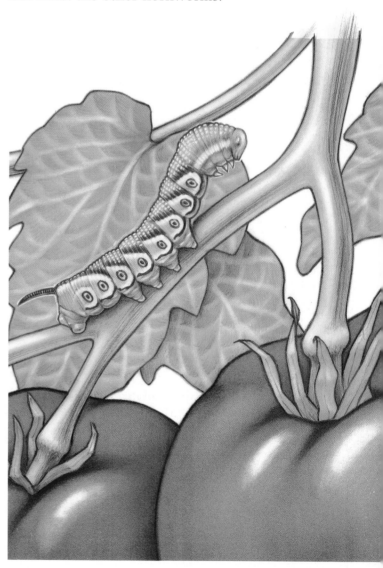

WHITEFLIES

Symptoms

Tiny winged insects feed on undersides of leaves. Leaves have spots of sticky, clear honeydew and may be mottled or turn yellow.

Hosts

Many vegetables and herbs.

Cure

Avoid the problem by attracting beneficial insects by growing small-flowered nectar plants, such as alyssum and dill. Use rowcovers (see page 145). Encourage natural enemies such as lacewing larvae and parasitoid wasps. For small infestations use yellow sticky traps, handpick or hose down plants with soapy water (see page 145). Spray plants with insecticidal soap or light horticultural oil when whiteflies are first noticed (see page 143). Be sure to spray both the tops and undersides of leaves. If infestation continues, use an insecticide containing azadirachtin, diazanon, pyrethrins or malathion (see pages 140-147). Make sure your plant is listed on the label.

WIREWORMS

Symptoms

Thin hard worms, $1^1/_2$ inches long, burrow inside of vegetable. Plants are stunted or grow slowly. Roots may be poorly formed.

Hosts

Many root crops, including carrot, potato and turnip.

Cure

Wood ashes provide a good natural control against wireworms. The larvae of click beetles feed on wireworms. Soil solarization can be effective in killing this worm (see page 150). Cultivate soil to expose wireworms to birds that eagerly eat the worms. Bury raw potato or carrot pieces several inches deep and dig them up every few days to collect larvae that feed on them. Apply insecticide-containing diazinon or chlorpyrifos to the soil prior to planting (see page 147). Work the insecticide into the top six to eight inches of the soil.

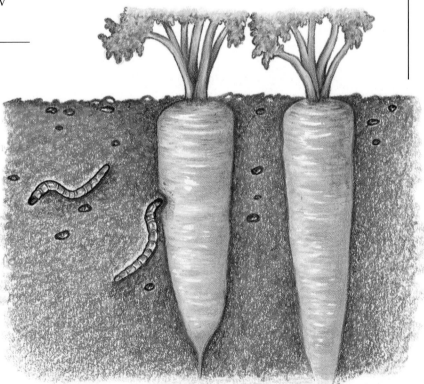

◖ CHAPTER 3 ◗
ENCYCLOPEDIA OF PLANTS

T his chapter contains detailed information on the diseases and pests most likely to attack specific vegetables and herbs. Here you'll find descriptions of the critters and diseases, the symptoms to look for, remedies for right now, and how to prevent problems in the future (if possible). Again, remedies begin with the ones gentlest to the environment and move on to more stringent methods.

Remember that whenever you use a product on a plant, you must read the label and follow directions to the letter if you want it to work for you *and* be as safe as possible to the environment.

ASPARAGUS
Asparagus officinalis

Asparagus is one of the few perennial plants in the vegetable garden. Because it is so long-lived, be sure to take extra care enriching the planting bed with plenty of compost and manure before planting.

Asparagus variety recommendations include the newer male hybrids in the "Jersey" series; gardeners in warm climates should look for the variety 'California 500', which does not require as much cool weather to produce a good crop of spears.

problem; combat by using drip irrigation. The fungus is present in decaying asparagus tissue, so do a thorough cleanup of the planting bed in fall to prevent this disease from recurring next year.

Asparagus Miners

Asparagus miners are small white worms that bore into asparagus stalks, sometimes causing a notched pattern on the stalks. Start by digging up and destroying infected spears. Avoid asparagus miners with the use of floating rowcovers (see page 145).

Cercospora Leaf Spot

A problem in warm, humid regions, this fungus disease shows up on the lower leaves of asparagus as gray or brownish oval spots, and gradually spreads up the plants. Overhead watering exacerbates this

Rust

The most common disease of asparagus is rust, which shows up as small yellow or orange-brown powdery spots or blisters on stems and foliage in summer. A fungicide containing captan, applied after the harvest, will help control future outbreaks (do not use during the harvest). Best bet is to avoid the problem altogether by planting rust-resistant asparagus varieties like 'Jersey Giant'.

Additional Pests:

Aphids, asparagus beetles, cutworms, fusarium wilt, gray mold, Japanese beetles, slugs and snails, spider mites and tarnished plant bugs will occasionally attack asparagus. Check the Quick Solution Chart on pages 36-61 for controls.

One of the harbingers of spring, asparagus is right at home with those other cool-weather-loving crops, cabbages and peas.

BASIL
Ocimum basilicum

Annual

All Zones

All basils thrive in a full sun location with fast-draining soil. Too much fertilizer will result in a profusion of leaves with a minimal flavor. For the most intense flavor, plants should be slightly stressed for water and nutrients, and picked just before they begin to flower.

Aphids

Aphids cluster in colonies, especially on new growth. These small, soft-bodied insects range in color from tan to green to brownish-black and secrete a sticky substance known as honeydew. The honeydew, in turn, attracts ants and eventually a dark, sooty mold. Avoid all these symptoms by getting rid of the aphids at the first sign of attack. Begin control by knocking the aphids off the foliage with a strong blast of water. If they persist, use an insecticidal soap (see page 143). Beneficial insects, such as lady beetles and lacewings, will help keep aphid populations under control (see pages 148-149); attract them with plantings of their favorite nectar plants, such as scabiosa, dill and yarrow.

Damping Off

This frustrating disease causes young seedlings to simply fall over and die. It's caused by a soil-borne fungus, particularly in heavy, poorly drained planting beds. Avoid the problem by incorporating plenty of organic matter into the soil to improve drainage and allow the bed to dry out slightly between waterings. Start the seed in a sterile soil mix and in clean containers. Improve air circulation around plants. Apply bottom heat to the seedling either by a heating pad or by setting the seedlings on top of the refrigerator. Do not seed basil outdoors until the soil has warmed up.

Basil 'Genovese' is the favored variety for making the classic sauce from Provence known as "pesto"—a combination of basil, garlic, pine nuts, Parmesan cheese and olive oil.

Once you start experimenting with basils, it's hard to stop. Here a combination of 'Opal' and 'Spicy Globe' share the spotlight. 'Spicy Globe' is one of the very attractive dwarf basils that combines great flavor with a neat, compact form: Perfect for creating a formal-looking edging.

The basil world is a large one, including some that are as ornamental as they are flavorful. 'Purple Ruffles' lives up to its name and makes an attractive garden partner with golden feverfew.

Slugs and Snails

If you wake up in the morning and find that something has eaten major portions of your basil's new growth and you see

'Thai' basil has a very distinctive flavor and appearance. An essential element in the cuisine of Thailand, this basil is frequently grown as much for its ornamental qualities as its culinary ones.

telltale slime trails—you'll know the culprits are slugs and/or snails. Although there are a number of more or less effective natural controls, even the most ardent organic gardeners have begun using a product called Escar-Go, which contains iron phosphate, a naturally occurring soil element (see page 144), to control these frustrating pests. Chemical controls include products (usually in bait form) containing metaldehyde (see page 147). Whether using Escar-Go or a chemical control, scatter it all around potential targets and any damp, shady spot where slugs and snails hide during the day. If you know there are slugs

and/or snails in your area, always treat your garden with a control before their damage is apparent; slugs and snails can do a tremendous amount of damage in even one night.

Additional Pests:

Fusarium wilt, grasshoppers and Japanese beetles will occasionally attack basil. Check the Quick Solution Chart on pages 36-61 for controls.

Gardeners have recently been introduced to exotic basil varieties from foreign lands. 'Basilico Finissimo a Palla' is a favorite Italian variety, equally at home in American soil.

BEANS
Phaseolus spp.

Annual   All Zones

Once beans start to mature, daily harvesting will prolong the harvest. Conversely, allow only a few beans to mature, and the plants will halt production.

Mosaic Virus

Bean mosaic virus shows up in crinkled leaves with odd-shaped spots of dark green and yellow. Best bet is to plant mosaic-virus-resistant varieties. There's no real control for this virus, but its effects can be lessened by controlling the insects which spread it, primarily aphids, with an insecticidal soap (see page 143). Chemical controls include insecticides containing diazinon or malathion (see page 147). Remove and destroy infected plants and do not save seed from infected plants.

Bush bean varieties, like 'EZ Gold', shown here, are easier to pick than pole bean varieties, but their crop tends to come in all at once rather than over a longer harvest period.

Bean Leaf Beetles

Bean leaf beetles eat $1/4$-inch holes in bean leaves, usually in a scattered pattern. The soil-borne larvae of these small, black-spotted, yellowish or red beetles will also eat the roots of bean plants. For small infestations you can handpick the beetles off the plants and dispose of them. Control with an application of beneficial nematodes (see page 149). Chemical controls include insecticides containing carbaryl or diazinon (see pages 146-147), paying particular attention to the undersides of leaves. A thorough cleanup of the planting bed in fall will help prevent these pests from returning next year.

One of the best of the flat-podded snap beans is the variety 'Romano'—a long-standing favorite with gardeners who also happen to be good cooks.

Serious gardeners are generally in agreement that the flat-podded snap bean varieties have more flavor than the round-podded types. The selection is somewhat limited, but includes the variety 'Sequoia', shown here.

Cercospora Leaf Spot

Different-sized spots on bean leaves, in shades of brown, black, purple or yellow are a sure sign of leaf spot. Best bet is to completely remove and destroy any affected plants at the first sign of attack. Avoid the problem by watering plants early in the day to

'Purple Dole' is one of the purple-podded bean varieties. It is favored by gardeners looking for the unusual and delicious.

allow foliage to dry before evening, and avoid wetting the foliage. Try to improve soil drainage. If you use pruning shears to remove diseased foliage, dip the blades in rubbing alcohol before reuse. Rotate crops to avoid reoccurance.

Gray Mold

A problem during extended periods of wet weather, gray mold shows up on the beans as a powdery, gray mold. There's not much you can do for this disease except prune off any affected pods or foliage, water plants in the morning, allow soil to dry out between waterings and pray for drier weather. Spray healthy foliage with a fungicide containing benomyl or chlorothalonil (see page 146). A thorough cleanup of the planting beds in fall will keep this malady from returning the following spring.

Powdery Mildew

Bean leaves, stems or flowers covered with a grayish-white powder are a sure sign of the disease known as powdery mildew. Damp, cool weather encourages powdery mildew, as do shady growing conditions. Cut off any damaged foliage (or whole plants) and discard. Space plants widely to encourage air circulation. Although it won't eradicate existing mildew, a

Snap beans are divided between round-podded and flat-podded varieties. Among the best of the round-podded types is the variety 'Goldkist'.

spray of baking soda will prevent future outbreaks (see page 141 for instructions on making the baking soda solution).

Additional Pests:

Anthracnose, cutworms, leafhoppers, Mexican bean beetle, rust and slugs will occasionally attack beans. Check the Quick Solution Chart on pages 36-61 for controls.

One of the great names in pole beans is the variety 'Kentucky Wonder', planted for generations and still favored by today's gardeners.

SAVING BEAN SEEDS

'Red Kidney', 'Marfax', 'Canada Red' dried beans.

Unlike snap beans, which are eaten when the pods and seeds are tender and basically immature, shell beans are all allowed to mature on the vine and then harvested. If you intend to store shell beans, leave them on the plants until the pods are fully dry and, when shaken, you can hear the beans rattle inside. The easiest way to harvest a shell bean crop is to pull up entire plants and hang them upside down in a dark, dry place to dry further. Then it's simply a matter of removing the pods and shucking the beans.

If you want to save shell bean seeds for use in next year's garden, be selective! Don't save seeds from undersized or diseased plants (diseases, such as anthracnose and bacterial blight, can be spread on bean seeds). Choose beans from the healthiest, most vigorous plants and make sure you label the collected seeds with the variety name.

Once the beans have been shucked from their pods, spread them out in a single layer on a screen in a warm, dry room, for two to three weeks, stirring them around every few days. Once thoroughly dry, pack the beans into clean, dry jars with tight-fitting lids. Freeze the bean-filled jars for 24 hours to kill any weevils and then store the beans in a cool dark place until you're ready to plant them the following spring.

'Pinto', 'Black Turtle', 'Pink' dried beans.

The dried seeds of bush beans.

BEE BALM
Monarda didyma,
M. citriodora, M. fistulosa

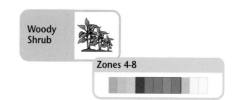

Woody Shrub

Zones 4-8

Slugs and Snails

If you wake up in the morning and find that something has eaten major portions of your bee balm's new growth and you see telltale slime trails—you'll know the culprits are slugs and/or snails. Edge plant containers with a copper strip barrier (see page 142). For small infestations you can handpick these pests and dispose of them. Place saucers of beer around plants as a trap for these pests. Although there are a number of more or less effective natural controls, even the most ardent organic gardeners have begun using a product called Escar-Go, which contains iron phosphate, a naturally occurring soil element (see page 144), to control these frustrating pests. Chemical controls include products (usually in bait form) containing metaldehyde (see page 147). Whether using Escar-Go or a chemical control, scatter it all around potential targets and any damp, shady spot where slugs and snails hide during the day. If you know there are slugs and/or snails in your area, always treat your garden with a control before their damage is apparent; slugs and snails can do a tremendous amount of damage in even one night.

Powdery Mildew

Bee balm leaves, stems or flowers covered with a grayish-white powder are a sure sign of the disease known as powdery mildew. Damp, cool weather encourages powdery mildew, as do shady growing conditions. Cut off any damaged foliage (or whole plants) and discard. Space plants widely to encourage air circulation. Although it won't eradicate existing mildew, a spray of baking soda will prevent future outbreaks (see page 141 for instructions on making the baking soda solution). At first sign of mildew spray plants with a horticultural oil (see page 143). Follow label instructions.

Rust

Shows up as small yellow or orange-brown powdery spots or blisters on stems and foliage in summer. A problem in humid, wet weather, begin control by pruning off and destroying any affected foliage. Space plants widely to encourage air circulation. A thorough cleanup of the planting beds in fall will keep this malady from returning the following spring.

Bee balm 'Cambridge Scarlet' provides great appeal for both gardeners as well as butterflies and hummingbirds.

BEETS
Beta vulgaris

Annual

All Zones

Beets grow best in a well-drained soil amended with plenty of organic matter and a nearly neutral pH. Use a light hand with fertilizer: Too much nitrogen will produce more leaves than roots.

For obvious reasons, the Italian heirloom beet 'Chioggia' is also known as 'Bull's-Eye Beet'.

Spinach Leaf Miners

The damage from these minute pests—the larvae of a fly—show up as light tan serpentine lines on beet leaves. Hard to control once the pests have mined their way into the leaves; best bet is to avoid the problem in the first place with the use of floating rowcovers (see page 145). For severe infestations spray the leaves with careful attention to the undersides with an insecticide containing malathion or diazanon (see page 147).

Additional Pests:

Aphids, flea beetles, root rot and scab occasionally attack beets. Check the Quick Solution Chart on pages 36-61 for controls.

Armyworms

Armyworms are really caterpillars, light green in color with darker stripes, anywhere from $1/2$ inch long to $1^1/2$ inches long. Armyworms do their damage at night, devouring beet foliage. Control with an application of Btk (see page 141).

Cercospora Leaf Spot

Different-sized spots on beet leaves, in shades of brown, black, purple or yellow, are a sign of leaf spot. Best bet is to completely remove and destroy any affected plants at the first sign of attack.

Avoid the problem by watering plants early in the day to allow foliage to dry before evening, and avoid wetting the foliage. If you use pruning shears to remove diseased foliage, dip the blades in rubbing alcohol before reuse.

'Golden' beets are among the most flavorful of any beet variety.

For consistent 1-inch-diameter slices, select one of the cylindrical beets such as 'Cylindra', shown here. Excellent for making pickled beets.

BROCCOLI
Brassica oleracea,
Botrytis group

Broccoli needs a rich, moist soil that has been amended with plenty of organic matter, and cool growing conditions. Once the weather turns hot and dry, broccoli will quickly go to seed.

Cabbage Loopers

These light green caterpillars, up to $1^1/2$ inches long, feed on the heads of broccoli; you can identify these pests by the distinctive way they loop up while crawling. The larvae of the gray moth, cabbage loopers usually appear in late spring. Make your garden inviting to birds to help control this pest. Start control by handpicking and destroying loopers. If infestation continues, spray with insecticidal soap or make an application of Btk (see page 141), or use an insecticide containing pyrethrum, rotenone, carbaryl or diazinon (see pages 144-147).

Cabbage Aphids

Cabbage aphids show up as clustered colonies of small tan, green or black insects, especially on new growth. Begin control by blasting aphids off foliage with a strong stream of water. If the problem persists, use an insecticidal soap, paying careful attention to the undersides of leaves where aphids can hide (see page 143).

Chemical controls include insecticides containing pyrethrum, diazinon or malathion (see page 147).

Club Root

This frustrating disease, caused by soil-borne fungus, causes broccoli plants to wilt during the day and recover at night. Unfortunately, the disease progresses, causing misshapen roots, and eventually kills the plant. Once infected, there is no cure; remove and destroy any infected plants at the first sign of attack. To help avoid the problem add agricultural lime (see page 144) to the planting bed until the soil pH reaches 7.0 or above. Rotate crops.

Fusarium Yellows

Fusarium yellows has symptoms similar to those of club root and can be controlled using the same methods (see above).

Living up to its name, the broccoli variety 'Super Dome' produces extremely large heads.

Additional Pests:

Cabbage maggots, damping off, downy mildew and cabbageworms will occasionally attack broccoli. Check the Quick Solution Chart on pages 36-61 for controls.

'Romanesco' broccoli produces unusual shaped heads in a unique shade of chartreuse. With its mild flavor, this variety is quickly becoming a favorite with garden gourmets.

Annual

All Zones

BRUSSELS SPROUTS
Brassica oleracea, *Gemmifera* group

Annual | All Zones

Like their cousin broccoli, Brussels sprouts require cool growing conditions and a rich, moist soil.

Fall Armyworms

Fall armyworms are dark caterpillars, approximately 1 inch long, which eat seedlings of Brussels sprouts plants at night, usually in late summer. For small infestations, handpick these pests and dispose of them. Control with an application of Btk (see page 141).

Imported Cabbageworms

Imported cabbageworms are yellow-striped, green caterpillars, approximately $1/2$ to $1^1/2$ inches long, which readily devour whole Brussels sprouts seedlings; will also eat irregular-shaped holes in leaves or tunnel directly into the Brussels sprouts' heads. Control with an application of Btk or insecticidal soap (see

pages 141 and 143). Other controls include insecticides containing pyrethrum, rotenone, carbaryl and diazinon (see page 144-147). Try companion-planting Brussels sprouts with radishes to reduce this pest.

Whiteflies

If you brush past Brussels sprouts and notice clouds of small white insects flying up, you have an infestation of whiteflies. Avoid the problem by attracting beneficial insects, such as lady beetles and tiny wasps with plantings of their favorite nectar plants, such as Queen-Anne's-lace, dill and yarrow. These pesky insects can also be controlled with insecticidal soap (see page 143).

Downy Mildew

Downy mildew is a disease prevalent in damp, cool weather. It shows up as a powdery, white coating on leaves. Remove any affected foliage or completely dig up and destroy any diseased plants at the first sign of attack. Some gardeners have reported success in avoiding downy mildew by the use of floating rowcovers, which evens out the growing temperatures (see page 150). Present damage cannot be eradicated but you can prevent future outbreaks with a fungicide containing maneb or cholothalonil (see pages 146-147). Be sure to clean up debris in the fall after harvest.

For the best flavor, allow Brussels sprouts to stay on the stem until after the first few frosts in fall.

CABBAGE
Brassica oleracea,
Capitata group

Cabbages grow best in a rich, moist soil, with a nearly neutral pH. They like the cool weather of spring and fall and, unlike most vegetables, can withstand temperatures down to 20°F.

Alternaria Leaf Spot

A problem in damp weather; cabbage leaves turn grayish and developed ring-shaped spots. Begin control by trimming off and disposing of infected leaves; if infection is severe, remove and dispose of entire plant. Help avoid the problem by allowing sufficient space between the plants to permit good air circulation.

Black Leg

If you notice dark-colored spots on the main stem of cabbages near the base of the plant, the problem is black leg. Plants eventually wilt and may die. Dig up and dispose of any infected plants. Help avoid the problem by allowing sufficient space between the

plants to permit good air circulation. Be sure to clean up plant debris in fall after harvest.

Homegrown cabbages (such as this 'Red Acre' variety) have much more flavor than store-bought cabbages.

'Chiefton Savoy' is the standard savoy cabbage, with densely curled, crumpled leaves.

Cabbage Loopers

These light green caterpillars, up to $1^1/2$ inches long, feed on the heads of cabbage; you can identify these pests by the distinctive way they loop up while crawling. The larvae of the gray moth, cabbage loopers usually appear in late spring. Make your garden attractive to birds that will help you control this pest. Start control by handpicking and destroying loopers. If infestation continues, spray with insecticidal soap or make an application of Btk (see page 141), or use an insecticide containing pyrethrum, rotenone, carbaryl or diazinon (see pages 144-147).

Cabbage Aphids

Cabbage aphids show up as clustered colonies of small tan, green or black insects, especially on new growth. Begin control by blasting aphids off foliage with a strong stream of water. If the problem persists, use an insecticidal soap, paying careful attention to the undersides of leaves where aphids can hide (see page 143). Chemical controls include insecticides containing pyrethrum, diazinon or malathion (see page 147).

Fusarium Yellows

This frustrating disease, caused by soil-borne fungus, causes cabbage plants to wilt during the day and recover at night. Unfortunately, the disease progresses, causing misshapen roots, and eventually kills the plant. Once infected, there is no cure; remove and destroy any infected plants at the first sign of attack. To help avoid the problem, add agricultural lime (see page 144) to the planting bed until the soil pH reaches 7.0 or above. Rotate crops.

Additional Pests:

Black rot, cabbage maggots and imported cabbageworms will occasionally attack cabbage. Check the Quick Solution Chart on pages 36-61 for controls.

Savoy cabbages, with their distinctive, crinkled leaves, are favored by many cooks for their flavor and texture.

CARROTS
Daucas carota var. *sativus*

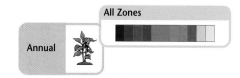

Annual   **All Zones**

Carrot Rust Fly Larvae

If you notice retarded, pale growth with your carrots, and reddish tunnels on the carrots themselves, the problem can be traced to the larvae of the carrot rust fly. The best control is to cover carrots with a floating rowcover (see page 145), to keep pests from infesting the crop in the first place. Plant resistant varieties.

Justly admired for their healthful properties, some carrot varieties are more blessed than others, such as this variety known as 'Juwarot Double Vitamin A'.

Parsley Worms

Missing or skeletonized carrot foliage indicates the presence of the 1- to 2-inch-long, white, green and black striped parsley worms, known for their menacing orange horns when aggravated. Because these beautiful worms develop into the even more beautiful black-and-yellow swallowtail butterfly, the best control is to cover carrots with a floating rowcover (see page 145), to keep pests from infesting the crop in the first place.

Carrots, like all other root crops, do best in a well-drained soil that is high in organic matter, with a nearly neutral pH.

If your soil is less than perfect, try growing carrots in raised beds filled with a loam soil. The results—whether you're growing mini-carrots or full-sized varieties—will be worth the extra effort.

One of the more unusual carrot varieties: 'Dragon Purple'.

Carrot Weevil Larvae

Unfortunately, there is no control for these white grubs that start feeding at the base of the carrot stem and work their way into the carrot itself. Pull up and discard any infected plants. The best control is to cover carrots with a floating rowcover (see page 145), to keep the carrots insect-free. Clean up garden debris in fall.

Alternaria Leaf Blight

A problem in damp weather, this disease shows up as dark spots on the oldish carrot foliage. Remove and dispose of any infected plants. Help avoid the problem by allowing sufficient space between the plants to permit good air circulation, and consider planting carrots in

'Sweet Sunshine' carrots, as their name suggests, have a delightful flavor and are the color of summer sunshine.

raised beds. Rotate crops, and plant resistant varieties.

Cercospora Leaf Spot

Different-sized spots on carrot leaves, in shades of brown, black, purple or yellow, are a sure sign of leaf spot. Best bet is to completely remove and destroy any affected plants at the first sign of attack. Avoid the problem by watering plants early in the day to allow foliage to dry before evening, and avoid wetting the foliage. If you use pruning shears to remove diseased foliage, dip the blades in rubbing alcohol before reuse. Rotate crops.

Root-Knot Nematodes

Characteristic nematode damage shows up as misshapen or forked, warty carrots. Either rotate your carrot planting to a different part of the garden each year or solarize the planting bed (see page 150).

Additional Pests:

Wireworms will occasionally attack carrots. Check the Quick Solution Chart on pages 36-61 for controls.

Carrots must be started from seed, so you might as well be adventurous when selecting varieties. Shown here, a Kuroda-type carrot known as 'Coral II F'.

CAULIFLOWER
Brassica oleracea,
Botrytis group

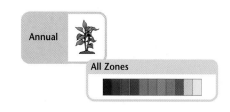

Annual

All Zones

Cauliflower demands cool weather. In most climates it's grown in the early spring or as a fall crop. Southern gardeners must grow it as a winter crop. Shown here, the variety 'Stardust'.

Black Leg

If you notice dark-colored spots on the main stem of cauliflowers, near the base of the plant, the problem is black leg. Plants eventually wilt and may die. Dig up and dispose of any infected plants. Help avoid the problem by allowing sufficient space between the plants to permit good air circulation.

Like other members of the cabbage family, cauliflower requires a well-drained soil rich in organic matter, and a neutral pH.

Downy Mildew

Downy mildew is a disease prevalent in damp, cool weather. It shows up as a powdery, white coating on leaves. Remove any affected foliage or completely dig up and destroy any diseased plants at the first sign of attack. Avoid the problem by watering plants early in the day so foliage has a chance to dry off before nightfall; space plants widely

To keep cauliflower heads pale and tender, they must be kept from the sun. Some varieties are "self-blanching", which means the leaves naturally grow up and around the head; others require the gardener to tie the leaves up around the heads by hand. Shown here, the variety 'Alverda'.

for increased air circulation. No fungicide will cure existing disease but will prevent future infection. Spray with a product containing maneb or chlorothalonil (see pages 146-147).

Club Root

This frustrating disease, caused by soil-borne fungus, causes cauliflower plants to wilt during the day and recover at night. Unfortunately, the disease progresses, causing misshapen roots, and eventually kills the plant. Once infected, there is no cure; remove and destroy any infected plants at the first sign of attack, and disinfect any tools with rubbing alcohol to prevent spreading the disease. To help avoid the problem, add agricultural lime (see page 144) to the planting bed until the soil pH reaches 7.0 or above. Rotate crops.

Additional Pests

Cabbage maggots and imported cabbageworms will occasionally attack cauliflower. Check the Quick Solution Chart on pages 36-61 for controls.

CELERY
Apium graveolens var. *dulce*

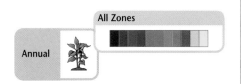

Annual

Carrot Rust Fly Larvae

If you notice retarded, pale, droopy growth with your celery, and reddish tunnels on the roots of the plant, the problem can be traced to the larvae of the carrot rust fly. The best control is to cover celery with a floating row-cover (see page 145), to keep pests from infesting the crop in the first place.

Cutworms

Cutworms, the soil-borne larvae of a variety of moths, are the bane of many gardeners. Particularly frustrating is the fact that cutworms prefer newly planted transplants and seedlings, cutting them off right at the base. For small infestations, handpick these pests and dispose of them. The best mechanical control is to form a paper collar (or cut off the bottom of a paper cup, or remove the top and bottom of an aluminum can) and place as protection around the plant. Introduce cutworm predators into the garden, such as beneficial soil nematodes, parasitoid wasps and tachinid flies (see page 149).

Soft Rot (Bacterial)

Luckily, this problem is fairly rare. In heavy, poorly drained soil—especially during extended periods of wet weather—the foliage of celery may start to rot. Because this condition can spread quickly, dig up and destroy any infected plants at the first sign of attack. Clean shovels and pruning shears used in removal with rubbing alcohol to prevent spreading the disease to healthy plants. To avoid the problem in the future, incorporate plenty of organic soil amendment to the beds to improve drainage. Rotate plantings.

Celery is a member of the parsley family. Even though it wasn't harvested as a food crop until the 1600s, celery can trace its roots back to ancient Mediterranean cultures, where it was used for medicinal purposes.

Celery needs a top-notch garden soil, well-drained and rich in organic matter. Two secrets for success: Keep the soil evenly moist and don't apply too much nitrogen fertilizer.

CHINESE CABBAGE
Brassica rapa,
Pekinensis group

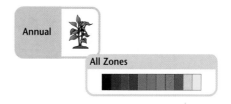

Annual

All Zones

In warm summer climates, it's best to grow Chinese cabbage as a fall crop, planted from seed in August. Even if frost (or snow!) hits early, you'll still get a good crop of greens.

Flea Beetles

Tiny bronze, black or brown beetles may be seen on the leaves of your Chinese cabbage, which are riddled with tiny holes; also the seedlings of your plant may dry out and die. A clean garden removes the home of the over-wintering adults, but you may avoid the problem of flea beetles by protecting seedlings with floating rowcovers (see page 145). White sticky traps, di-atomaceous earth and para-sitic nematodes are helpful in controlling these pests (see page 149). Chemical controls of insecticidal soap, or sprays con-taining the insecticide carbaryl or rotenone may be used if needed (see pages 144 and 146).

Slugs and Snails

If you wake up in the morn-ing and find that something has eaten major portions of your bee balm's new growth and you find telltale slime trails—you'll know the culprits are slugs and/or snails. For light infesta-tions, handpick these pests and dispose of them. Place saucers of beer around plants to create traps. Sprinkle diatomaceous earth around plants (see page 142). Although there are a number of more or less effec-tive natural controls, even the most ardent organic gardeners have begun using a product called Escar-Go, which contains iron

'Kasumi' is one of the many Chinese-type cabbages. Like their European counterparts, Chinese cab-bages are cool-weather crops, best grown in the early spring and fall in most climates.

Devoted gardeners go the extra step in ensuring a long cabbage harvest. How? Just replant a garden-grown crop into pots for "fresh" storage in the root cellar.

phosphate, a naturally occurring soil element (see page 144), to control these frustrating pests. Chemical controls include products (usually in bait form) containing metaldehyde (see page 147). Whether using Escar-Go or a chemical control, scatter it all around potential targets and any damp, shady spot where slugs and snails hide during the day. If you know there are slugs and/or snails in your area, always treat your garden with a control before their damage is apparent; slugs and snails can do a tremendous amount of damage in even one night.

Downy Mildew

Downy mildew is a disease prevalent in damp, cool weather. It shows up as a powdery, white coating on leaves. Remove any affected foliage or completely dig up and destroy any diseased plants at the first sign of attack. Avoid the problem by watering plants early in the day so foliage has a chance to dry off before nightfall; space plants widely for increased air circulation. No fungicide will cure existing disease but will prevent future infection. Spray with a product containing maneb or chlorothalonil (see pages 146-147).

'Blues', another Chinese cabbage, is an unusual variety sought out by lovers of Asian cuisine.

CORIANDER, CILANTRO
Coriandrum sativum

Annual

All Zones

It's a case of split personality in the garden: The name "coriander" refers to the seed of the cilantro plant, while the leafy portion is called "cilantro." Shown here are coriander seeds.

year to the next. If it's been a problem before, try planting coriander in a different garden location. At the first sign of attack, make an application of liquid fertilizer; the resulting boost in growth may keep the plants from succumbing to the disease. Rotate plantings.

Bacterial Wilt

If your coriander suddenly wilts, even though there's sufficient moisture in the soil, bacterial wilt is the probable cause—especially if there's been an extended period of warm weather. Use floating rowcovers to exclude insect pests. Dig up and destroy any infected plants at the first sign of attack. Remove all soil the roots have touched. Avoid problems in the future by incorporating plenty of organic matter into the planting beds, and keep them free of garden debris. Maximize air circulation by not overcrowding plants.

Powdery Mildew

Coriander leaves and stems covered with a grayish-white powder are a sure sign of the disease known as powdery mildew. Damp, cool weather encourages powdery mildew, as do shady growing conditions. Cut off any damaged foliage (or whole plants) and discard. Although existing damage cannot be eliminated, future outbreaks of powdery mildew can be prevented with a baking soda spray (see page 141).

Verticillium Wilt

Verticillium wilt will cause coriander foliage to turn yellow with brown blotches. Portions of the plant may wilt suddenly. A fungus disease, verticillium wilt lives in garden soil from one

An essential flavor note in Asian and Mexican cuisines, there's simply no middle ground when it comes to cilantro: either you can't get enough of it, or you never want to taste it again.

Cilantro prefers the cool weather of early spring and fall; long, hot days will cause it to quickly "bolt" (go to seed). Varieties such as 'Slow Bolt' show less of this trait, but nonetheless, do best in cool temperatures.

CORN
Zea mays

Annual — All Zones

Birds and Mice

See pages 22-29 for control of these pests, which eat the kernels of corn right out of the soil, even before they have a chance to germinate.

Corn Rootworms

Corn rootworms are the larvae of small beetles that eat the roots of corn plants, halting their development. Pull and destroy any infected plants; don't plant corn in the same location for at least two years or avoid the problem in the future by making an application of beneficial nematodes (see page 149). Corn rootworms can be controlled at planting time with a soil application of an insecticide containing diazinon (see page 147). Adult beetles chew on corn foliage, as well as the silks and tassels, and can be controlled with the dust form of the insecticide carbaryl (see page 146). Rotate crops.

Maize Dwarf Mosaic Virus and Maize Chlorotic Dwarf Virus

Maize dwarf mosaic virus and maize chlorotic dwarf virus produce distorted or oddly colored corn foliage. The problem can be partially avoided by planting corn as early as possible in the growing season, but best bet is to plant resistant varieties.

Good cooks know to put the kettle on to boil before going out to harvest fresh, sweet corn. The shorter the time between the garden and table, the better the flavor.

All corn varieties, including 'Mohawk Blue', shown here, are "hungry" crops that require a well-drained soil loaded with nutrients.

Northern Corn Leaf Blight

Northern corn leaf blight shows up as large grayish-green spots or streaks on corn leaves, sometimes up to six inches long. Best bet is to plant resistant corn varieties.

Southern Corn Leaf Blight

This fungal disease makes its appearance with small, light brown, red-ringed oval spots. This disease is exacerbated by cool weather. Best bet is to plant resistant corn varieties.

Stewart's Bacterial Wilt

Stewart's bacterial wilt is caused by flea beetles and is a particular problem when mild winters allow the beetles to survive from one growing season to the next. They are also encouraged by weeds growing near the corn; keep weedy areas mowed or cleared. Damage appears when corn plants are young, with grayish or yellow-

Corn, along with potatoes and squash, is one of the New World's major contributions to world food.

ish streaks in the foliage; once stems darken at their base, plants usually die. Best bet is to plant resistant corn varieties. At the first sign of attack, spray corn with insecticidal soap (see page 143). Other controls include insecticides that contain rotenone or carbaryl (see pages 144 and 146).

Additional Pests:

Corn earworms, cutworms, European corn borers and rust will occasionally attack corn. Check the Quick Solution Chart on pages 36-61 for controls.

Ornamental or 'Indian' corn is one of this country's favorite reminders of the joys of the harvest season.

'Silver Queen' is the standard white sweet corn against which all other white corn varieties are measured.

CUCUMBERS
Cucumis sativus

Annual

All Zones

Native to the East Indies, cucumbers are tropical plants grown as annuals. While they crave a rich soil, too much nitrogen will result in all foliage and no fruit.

Squash Vine Borers

The damage from these 1-inch-long white worms, which actually bore right into cucumber stems, shows up with wilted foliage. Use floating rowcovers to protect plants in the first place (see page 145). There's not much the gardener can do once the worm has entered the protection of the stem. You can either prune away the affected part of the plant or make a slit in the stem where you notice a sawdust-like material (called frass), and remove the worm, taping the stem back together again.

Additional Pests:

Anthracnose, bacterial wilt, cutworms and downy mildew occasionally attack cucumbers. Check the Quick Solution Chart on pages 36-61 for controls.

Alternaria Blight

A problem in damp weather, this disease shows up as dark spots on the cucumber foliage. Remove and dispose of infected foliage or entire plants. Help avoid the problem by allowing sufficient space between the plants to permit good air circulation.

There's no point in planting cucumbers before your soil is thoroughly warm; if it's too cool, the seeds or seedlings will just sit in the soil and sulk, and may even rot away. Shown here, the variety 'Cool Breeze'.

Cucumber Mosaic Virus

Cucumber mosaic virus damages cucumber foliage to the point where it looks like the plant is dying. Leaves are distorted, with yellow and dark green blotches, and may become brittle. Pull out infected plants. The best control is to cover cucumbers with a floating rowcover (see page 145), to keep the insects that transmit this virus from infecting the crop in the first place. If you've had problems with this virus in the past, favor resistant cucumber varieties (see pages 19-21).

Although it is usually eaten fresh, the yellow 'Lemon' cucumber makes excellent pickles if harvested when small.

DILL
Anethum graveolens

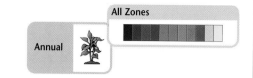

Annual — All Zones

'Fernleaf' dill is an unusual dwarf variety which grows about 18 inches tall and produces bushy plants with numerous side shoots.

Native to the Mediterranean and southern Russia, dill is still strongly associated with the foods of these regions.

Aphids

Aphids, those masses of small tan, green or black insects, sometimes congregate on the new growth of dill plants. Attract beneficial insects like lady beetles and lacewings by planting small-flowered nectar plants. Start control by knocking aphids off with a strong blast of water. If they persist, use an insecticidal soap or azadirachtin (see pages 140 and 143). Chemical controls include products that contain diazinon or malathion (see page 147).

Parsley Worms

Missing or skeletonized dill foliage indicates the presence of the 1- to 2-inch-long, white, green and black striped parsley worms, known for their menacing orange horns when aggravated. Because these beautiful worms develop into the even more beautiful black-and-yellow swallowtail butterfly, the best control is to cover dill with a floating rowcover (see page 145), to keep pests from infesting the crop in the first place, or just plant extra dill plants for these extraordinary garden visitors.

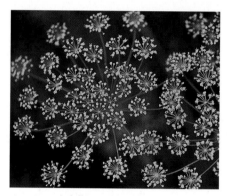

An essential flavor ingredient for canning and pickling, the flower heads of dill are at their peak when they have just begun to open.

Mosaic

There's no control once this malady affects dill; it produces stunted and deformed foliage. Remove and destroy infected plants. You can avoid this viral disease by covering the dill with floating rowcovers to exclude the sap-sucking insects (see page 145) that spread the disease. Attract beneficial insects by planting small-flowered nectar plants, such as yarrow and Queen-Anne's-lace.

'Bouquet' dill will grow 3 or 4 feet tall and produce plenty of aromatic foliage over a long season.

EGGPLANT
Solanum melongena var. *esculentum*

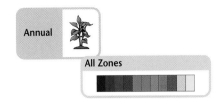

Annual

All Zones

Eggplants are thought to have originated in Southeast Asia. Eggplants eventually found their way to America in the 17th century, after being introduced to Europe in the late Middle Ages.

Americans are still being introduced to new varieties of eggplant, such as the wonderful 'Violette di Firenze' from Italy.

Verticillium Wilt

Verticillium wilt will cause eggplant foliage to turn yellow with brown blotches. Portions of the plant may wilt suddenly. A fungus disease, verticillium wilt lives in garden soil from one year to the next. If it's been a problem before, try planting eggplant in a different garden location. At the first sign of attack, make an application of liquid fertilizer; the resulting boost in growth may keep the plants from succumbing to the disease.

Additional Pests:

Blister beetles and flea beetles will occasionally attack eggplant. Check the Quick Solution Chart on pages 36-61 for controls.

Another recent introduction from Italy—a land that loves its eggplant— 'Listada di Gandia'.

Early Blight

Early blight is a fungal disease spread by wind and rain. Damage shows up as darkish spots on older leaves. There is no control once plants are infected with this disease; simply remove and destroy infected plants. Avoid the problem in the future by planting eggplant in a different garden location, by spacing plants generously to provide good air circulation and by planting in raised beds.

FENNEL
Foeniculum vulgare

All Zones

Annual

Good cooks admire the licorice flavor of fennel as the perfect accompaniment for any fish dish.

Parsley Worms

Chewed or missing fennel foliage indicates the presence of the 1- to 2-inch-long, white, green and black striped parsley worms, known for their menacing orange horns when aggravated. Because these beautiful worms develop into the even more beautiful black-and-yellow swallowtail butterfly, the best control is to cover

The so-called Florence fennel is grown for its swollen bulb-like base rather than its foliage. It shares the licorice flavor of all fennels.

dill with a floating rowcover (see page 145), to keep pests from infesting the crop in the first place, or just plant extra fennel plants for these extraordinary garden visitors.

Aphids

Aphids, those masses of small tan, green or black insects, sometimes congregate on the new growth of fennel. Start control by knocking aphids off with a strong blast of water. Encourage aphid-attacking insects by planting small-flowered nectar plants, such as scabiosa, Queen-Anne's-lace or yarrow. If they persist, use an insecticidal soap or azadirachtin (see pages 140 and 143). Chemical controls include products which contain diazinon or malathion.

'Smoky', one of the bronze-colored fennels, is valued as much for its ornamental qualities as its flavor.

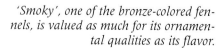

GARLIC
Allium sativum

Annual

All Zones

Keep garlic growing steadily throughout the summer. When the tops start to whither and turn yellow, dig the bulbs and cure them in a sunny, dry spot for three days. Once cured, store bulbs in a dark, cool, dry place.

If you think of garlic as the bulb it is, you'll have a clue to its best planting time: Just like spring-flowering bulbs, the best time to plant is early enough in fall so the bulbs can begin to form roots, but late enough so that the growing tip of the plant won't emerge and be damaged by cold winter temperatures. Shown here, the variety 'Nootka Rose'.

Onion Maggots

Onion maggots are the small ($1/3$-inch-long) soil-borne larvae of the onion maggot fly. These damaging grubs bore directly into the garlic cloves, destroying the crop. Best bet is to avoid the problem altogether by using floating row-covers to exclude the onion maggot flies before they can lay their eggs (see page 145). Avoid the problem in the future with an application of beneficial nematodes (see page 149). Chemical controls include insecticides containing diazinon or chlorpyrifos, applied to the soil at planting time (see page 147).

Blue and White Rot

Blue mold rot and white rot keep the garlic crop from maturing, showing up as blue spots on immature, fallen garlic foliage or yellow tips. Although there is no control, avoid the problem by rotating garlic plantings in different garden plots each year, and by being careful not to damage cloves when separating for planting. Some help is provided by planting garlic in raised beds.

Garlic falls into two types—hardneck and softneck. The stems of hardneck type, such as the one shown here: dry hard in the center; tend to have fewer cloves but more pungent flavor; they are also thicker, and more easily peeled. But hardnecks only keep in storage for 3 or 4 months. Softneck garlic varieties are milder and can be successfully stored for up to a year.

KALE
Brassica oleracea, Acephala group

All Zones

Annual

Cabbage Loopers

These light green caterpillars, up to 1¹/₂ inches long, feed on kale; you can identify these pests by the distinctive way they loop up while crawling. The larvae of the gray moth, cabbage loopers usually appear in late spring. Start control by handpicking and destroying loopers. Make your garden attractive to birds to help control this pest. If infestation continues, spray with insecticidal soap or make an application of Btk (see page 141), or use an insecticide containing pyrethrum, rotenone, carbaryl or diazinon (see pages 144-147).

Whiteflies

If you brush past a kale plant and you notice clouds of small white insects flying up, you have an infestation of whiteflies. Use floating rowcovers to exclude this pest (see page 145). Encourage beneficial insects such as lady beetles and tiny wasps by planting small-flowered nectar plants, such as dill or yarrow. These pesky insects can be controlled with insecticidal soap or azadirachtin (see pages 140 and 143). Chemical controls include products containing malathion, carbaryl or diazinon (see pages 146-147).

'Red Bor' salad kale, one of the "dual-purpose" kales that are both edible and ornamental.

Fall Armyworms

Fall armyworms are dark caterpillars, approximately 1 inch long, which eat seedlings of kale plants at night, usually in late summer. For small infestations handpick the worms and dispose of them. Control with an application of Btk (see page 141).

Cabbage Aphids

Cabbage aphids show up as clustered colonies of small tan, green or black insects, especially on new growth. Begin control by blasting aphids off foliage with a strong stream of water. If the problem persists, use an insecticidal soap, paying careful attention to the undersides of leaves where aphids can hide

(see page 143). Chemical controls include insecticides containing pyrethrum, diazinon or malathion (see page 147).

Additional Pests:

Damping off, downy mildew and imported cabbageworms will occasionally attack kale. Check the Quick Solution Chart on pages 36-61 for controls.

Kales, and their close relatives, collards, are essentially nonheading cabbages and are the easiest members of the family to grow.

Although considered ornamental, kale varieties such as 'Fiesta' and 'Red Chidon' are edible but not as tasty as their nonshowy cousins.

KOHLRABI
Brassica oleracea,
Gongylodes group

All Zones

Annual

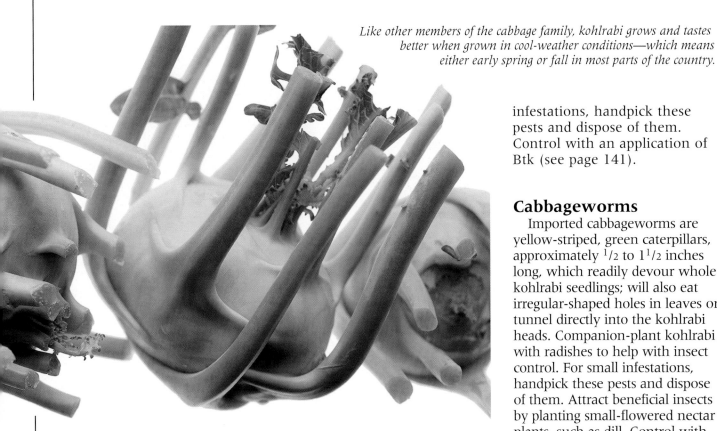

Like other members of the cabbage family, kohlrabi grows and tastes better when grown in cool-weather conditions—which means either early spring or fall in most parts of the country.

Cabbage Loopers

These light green caterpil-lars, up to $1^1/2$ inches long, feed on kohlrabi; you can iden-tify these pests by the distinc-tive way they loop up while crawling. The larvae of the gray moth, cabbage loopers usually appear in late spring. Start control by handpicking and destroying loopers. Make your garden attractive to birds to help control the pest. For a small infestation, handpick these pests and dispose of them. If infestation continues, spray with insecticidal soap or make an application of Btk (see page 141), or use an insecticide containing pyrethrum, rotenone, car-baryl or diazinon (see pages 144-147).

Fall Armyworms

Fall armyworms are dark caterpillars, approximately 1 inch long, which eat seedlings of kohlrabi plants at night, usu-ally in late summer. For small

Kohlrabi is a quick-growing member of the cabbage family. Popular in central Europe for centuries, kohlrabi's mild flavor is now winning favor in this country. Both white and purple vari-eties are available.

infestations, handpick these pests and dispose of them. Control with an application of Btk (see page 141).

Cabbageworms

Imported cabbageworms are yellow-striped, green caterpillars, approximately $1/2$ to $1^1/2$ inches long, which readily devour whole kohlrabi seedlings; will also eat irregular-shaped holes in leaves or tunnel directly into the kohlrabi heads. Companion-plant kohlrabi with radishes to help with insect control. For small infestations, handpick these pests and dispose of them. Attract beneficial insects by planting small-flowered nectar plants, such as dill. Control with an application of Btk or insectici-dal soap (see page 141). Other controls include insecticides con-taining pyrethrum, rotenone, car-baryl and diazinon (see pages 144-147).

Damping Off

This frustrating disease causes young seedlings to simply fall over and die. It's caused by a soil-borne fungus, particularly in heavy, poorly drained planting beds. Use sterile seed starting mix and clean containers. Avoid the problem by incorpo-rating plenty of organic matter into the soil to im-prove drainage and allow the bed to dry out slightly between waterings.

LAVENDER
Lavandula spp.

Cercospora Leaf Spot

Different-sized spots on lavender leaves, in shades of brown, black, purple or yellow, are a sure sign of leaf spot. Best bet is to completely remove and destroy any affected plants at the first sign of attack. Avoid the problem by watering plants early in the day to allow foliage to dry before evening, and avoid wetting the foliage. If you use pruning shears to remove diseased foliage, dip the blades in rubbing alcohol before reuse.

Fusarium Wilt

Fusarium wilt is a frustrating soil-borne disease that causes lavender plants to turn yellow or individual leaves to turn brown, eventually killing the

A perennial favorite in the herb garden, lavender has been grown for both medicinal and culinary uses since ancient times.

French lavender (Lavandula dentata), as shown here, has foliage with scalloped edges; English lavender has smooth-edged leaves.

plant. Avoid the problem by incorporating plenty of leaf mold or peat moss into the soil to improve soil drainage. Do not overwater plants, and make sure to plant lavender in a sunny spot. If fusarium wilt attacks, completely remove and discard the affected plant, along with any soil the roots have come into contact with. If fusarium wilt has previously been a problem, plant lavender in another location. If practical, solarizing the soil (see page 150) will control soil-borne diseases.

Spanish lavender (Lavandula stoechas) has large, showy flower bracts.

Root-Knot Nematode

Characteristic nematode damage shows up as yellowed, stunted foliage and when the plant is removed from the soil, you'll notice misshapen or forked, warty roots. Either rotate your lavender plantings to a different part of the garden each year or solarize the planting bed (see page 150).

LEEKS
Allium ampeloprasum,
Porrum group

Annual | All Zones

For success with leeks, provide them with a deeply worked soil that is rich in organic matter. The soil should be well drained, as leeks require more or less constant moisture but cannot tolerate standing water.

Thrips

The damage from these tiny insects shows up as silvery streaking on leaves and distorted new growth. Begin control by knocking thrips off foliage with a strong blast of water. Clean up any weeds around plants. If the problem persists, use an insecticidal soap or azadirachtin (see pages 140 and 143). Chemical controls include products containing carbaryl, malathion or diazinon (see pages 146-147).

Onion Maggots

Onion maggots are the small (1/3-inch-long) soil-borne larvae of the onion maggot fly. These damaging grubs bore directly into the bases of leeks, effectively destroying the crop. Best bet is to avoid the problem altogether by using floating rowcovers to exclude the onion maggot flies before they can lay their eggs (see page 145). Avoid the problem in the future with an application of beneficial nematodes (see page 149). Chemical controls include insecticides containing diazinon

'Blue Solaise' leeks, pictured here, are among the most popular leek varieties. Others include 'King Richard' and 'Nebraska'.

or chlorpyrifos, applied to the soil at planting time (see page 147).

Fusarium Basal Rot

Fusarium basal rot shows up with yellow tips on leek foliage, which may completely wilt away; when plants are dug, roots will be rotted. Dig up and destroy any affected plants at the first sign of attack. To avoid the problem, control onion maggots (see page 53), rotate leek plantings in different garden plots each year or grow in raised beds. Plant healthy bulbs.

Additional Pests:

Pink root occasionally attacks leeks. Check the Quick Solution Chart on pages 36-61 for controls.

Lemon Balm
Melissa officinalis

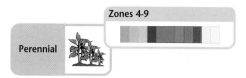

Zones 4-9

Perennial

Fusarium Wilt

Fusarium wilt is a frustrating soil-borne disease which causes lemon balm plants to turn yellow, or individual leaves to turn brown, eventually killing the plant. Avoid the problem by incorporating plenty of leaf mold or peat moss into the soil to improve soil drainage. If fusarium wilt attacks, completely remove and discard the affected plant, along with any soil the roots have come into contact with. If fusarium wilt has previously been a problem, plant lemon balm in another location. If practical, solarizing the soil (see page 150) will control soil-borne diseases.

Powdery Mildew

Lemon balm foliage that is covered with a powdery white substance indicates the presence of the disease known as powdery mildew. While it doesn't kill the plants, it can render them so unattractive that gardeners wish the plants would die. Begin control by cutting off and discarding any affected foliage. Although existing damage cannot be eliminated, future outbreaks

A member of the vast mint family, lemon balm is a perennial herb with a refreshing lemon fragrance. The flavor has an underlying hint of mint.

of powdery mildew can be prevented with a baking soda spray (see page 141).

Rust

Orange-brown, powdery spots on the foliage indicate the presence of the disease known as rust. Since it is encouraged by damp weather and damp leaves, you can help control rust by watering plants early in the day to allow foliage to dry off before nightfall; avoid, if possible, any water on the foliage. Most attacks of rust on lemon balms can be controlled by simply cutting off and discarding affected foliage, especially if you catch the disease early on.

Variegated forms of lemon balm may be sold as 'Variegata' or 'Aurea'. A variety with pure, bright yellow foliage is sold by the name of 'Allgold'.

LEMON VERBENA
Aloysia triphylla

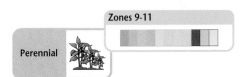

Perennial

Zones 9-11

Spider Mites

Spider mites often attack plants stressed by lack of water. Leaves will appear speckled, along with minute webbing; affected foliage will eventually turn yellow and drop. Avoid spider mites by keeping plants well watered. Control by spraying infested foliage with a strong blast of water. If the problem persists, spray with insecticidal soap or light horticultural oil (see page 143).

Verbena, with its lemony scent and flavor, is often used to perfume soaps, bath oils and other cosmetics. Cooks like the light, citrusy flavor it adds to cold drinks, jellies and all manner of baked goods. Because the leaves may be tough, they should be very finely chopped before adding to food.

LETTUCE
Lactuca sativa

Annual

Crisphead types of lettuce include the familiar "iceberg" varieties, as well as not-so-familiar ones like this red form known as 'Red Iceberg'.

Romaine lettuce, such as the 'Medallion' and 'Cimmaron' varieties pictured here, is a necessary ingredient for "Caesar" salads.

Botrytis

Botrytis is rarely a problem with lettuce, except during periods of extended rain. Seedlings will wilt and simply rot away, sometimes showing areas of gray mold. Existing damage cannot be remedied, but avoid future infection with a spray of baking soda (see page 141).

Bottom Rot

Bottom rot is a fungal disease that affects the older leaves of lettuce, primarily heading types with leaves close to the soil. The fungus causes lower leaves to turn brown and rot. There's no cure, except to rotate lettuce plantings to different plots in the garden, or to favor leaf lettuces, with their upright habit.

Mosaic Virus

Lettuce mosaic virus and cucumber mosaic virus show up with new lettuce growth

diminished in size; may show brown and yellow streaks, as well. These damage lettuce foliage to the point where it looks like the plant is dying. The best control is to cover lettuce with a floating rowcover

(see page 145), to keep the insects which transmit this virus from infecting the crop in the first place. If you've had problems with this virus in the past, favor resistant lettuce varieties (see pages 19-21).

Additional Pests:

Aphids, cutworms and damping off will occasionally attack lettuce. Check the Quick Solution Chart on pages 36-61 for controls.

Romaine lettuces produce upright-growing plants with thick leaves. Both green and red varieties, such as the one known as 'Outrageous', shown here, are available.

LOVAGE
Levisticum officinale

Perennial

Zones 5-8

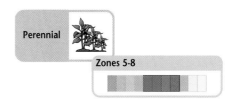

A lovage plant, which tastes like celery, may grow to over six feet tall. When in bloom, lovage is as prized for its ornamental qualities as its culinary ones. And lovage makes a great candidate for the back of a perennial border.

Aphids

Aphids, those masses of small tan, green or black insects, sometimes congregate on the new growth of lovage. Start control by knocking aphids off with a strong blast of water. If they persist, use an insecticidal soap or azadirachtin (see pages 140 and 143). Attract beneficial insects such as lady beetles and lacewings (see pages 148-149) by planting small-flowered nectar plants like dill, fennel and yarrow. Chemical controls include products that contain diazinon or malathion (see page 147).

Leaf Miners

Light brown trails in lovage leaves are the telltale marks of serpentine leaf miners—tiny larvae that burrow inside the leaves. Use floating rowcovers to exclude pest (see page 145). Control by cutting off and discarding any affected foliage. Prevent future infestations with a soil application of beneficial nematodes (see page 149).

MARJORAM
Origanum majorana

All Zones

Annual

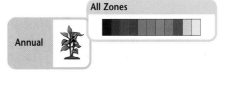

Marjoram grows up to 2¹/₂ feet tall. For the best production of leaves, keep flowers trimmed off and regularly prune the plant to prevent woodiness. Marjoram will grow as a perennial in mild winter climates; elsewhere, pot up garden-grown plants in the fall and move them indoors to a sunny windowsill for the winter.

Spider Mites

Spider mites often attack plants stressed by lack of water. Leaves will appear speckled, along with minute webbing; affected foliage will eventually turn yellow and drop. Avoid spider mites by keeping plants well watered. Control by spraying infested foliage with a strong blast of water. Attract beneficial insects with small-flowered nectar plants, such as yarrow and dill. If the problem persists, spray with insecticidal soap or light horticultural oil (see page 143).

Members of the marjoram family (relatives of mint) include Crete dittany, sweet marjoram (shown here) and oregano or wild marjoram. Marjoram, with its sweet, pungent flavor and slight mint aftertaste, has been a culinary favorite since ancient times.

MELONS
Cucumis melo

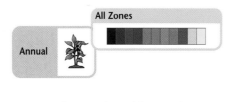

All Zones

Annual

Cucumber Beetles

Striped (or spotted) cucumber beetles are small ($1/4$- to $1/3$-inch-long) beetles that don't do much damage initially, but may transmit bacterial wilt—a fatal disease for melons. First sign of attack from these beetles shows up with irregular holes chewed in leaves. Begin control by hand-picking and destroying beetles. Use floating rowcover to exclude insects (see page 145). If infestation persists, spray with insecticide containing pyrethrum, diazinon or carbaryl (see pages 146-147).

Powdery Mildew

Melon leaves, stems or flowers covered with a grayish-white powder are a sure sign of the disease known as powdery mildew. Damp, cool weather encourages powdery mildew, as do shady growing conditions. Cut off any damaged foliage (or whole plants) and discard. Be sure to rotate crops and space plants for

Melons, such as this cantaloupe type known as 'French Orange', require a full-sun location and a soil rich in organic matter. Keep the soil well nourished, but be aware that too much nitrogen will result in huge, leafy plants with very few fruits.

good air circulation. Although existing damage cannot be eliminated, future outbreaks of powdery mildew can be prevented with a sulfur spray (see page 145). Treat plants with fungicide containing chlorothalonil (see page 146).

Alternaria Blight

A problem in damp weather, this disease shows up as dark spots on the melon foliage. Remove and dispose of infected foliage or entire plants. Help avoid the problem by allowing sufficient space between the plants to permit good air circulation.

Mosaic Viruses

There's no control once this malady affects melons; it produces stunted and deformed foliage, sometimes showing dark green blotches. Remove and destroy infected plants. You can avoid this viral disease by covering the melons with floating rowcovers to exclude the sap-sucking insects that spread the disease.

Additional Pests:

Bacterial wilt, flea beetles, scab and squash vine borers will occasionally attack melon. Check the Quick Solution Chart on pages 36-61 for controls.

All melons, including the 'Banana' variety pictured here, should have a consistent supply of water until the fruit reaches four or so inches in diameter. After that, discontinue watering to concentrate the flavors of the melon. Mulch heavily with an organic material to help keep the existing soil moisture level adequate.

For maximum flavor, harvest cantaloupes, such as the 'Honey Girl' variety shown here, when the melon separates from the vine with the slightest of tugs—a state of ripeness known as "full slip."

MINT
Mentha spp.

Zones 4-9

Perennial

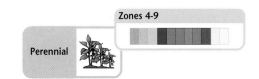

All members of the mint family, such as the spearmint pictured here, are extremely easy to grow and produce great quantities of pungent foliage. This harvest is being dried for use in making spearmint tea.

Four-Lined Plant Bugs

Four-lined plant bugs cause dark spots on foliage, which may drop. About the only control is to handpick and destroy these $^1/_3$-inch-long bugs with black-striped wings.

Caterpillars

Caterpillars may occasionally chew on the edges of mint leaves. These 1-inch-long, fuzzy caterpillars turn into beautiful butterflies, so best bet is to simply plant extra mint to share with them, or handpick and place in a different part of the garden.

Verticillium Wilt

Verticillium wilt will cause mint foliage to turn yellow with brown blotches. Portions of the plant may wilt suddenly. A fungus disease, verticillium wilt lives in garden soil from one year to the next. If it's been a problem before, try planting mint in a different garden location. At the first sign of attack, make an application of liquid fertilizer; the resulting boost in growth may keep the plants from succumbing to the disease.

Additional Pests:

Aphids and rust will occasionally attack mint. Check the Quick Solution Chart on pages 36-61 for controls.

Pineapple mint (Mentha suaveolens 'Variegata'), is an attractive plant with variegated foliage scented with the fragrance of pineapple.

Peppermint (Mentha piperita) is a strongly scented mint that will produce a bushy plant up to three feet tall.

OKRA
Abelmoschus esculentus

Annual  All Zones

Root-Knot Nematodes

Characteristic nematode damage causes okra to grow slowly, probably exhibiting wilted foliage even when adequate moisture is present in the soil. Either rotate your okra plantings to a different part of the garden each year, or solarize the planting bed (see page 150) or treat with chitin (see page 141). Rotate planting with marigolds and turn the plants under at the end of the season as marigolds have a nematode-inhibiting effect on the soil.

Blossom Blight

Blossom blight affects the okra flowers with various-colored, dotted mold, most prevalent during periods of humid or rainy weather. No cure, save for simply removing and destroying infected foliage. Provide generous space between plants to promote good air circulation.

Whether red or green, okra needs a full-sun location, a fast-draining soil rich in organic matter and plenty of long, warm days.

Southern Blight

Southern blight is a problem for okra planted in warm climates. Whole plants rot at the base and strange webbing or fungus strings form on the soil in the presence of this disease. Avoid this problem by planting okra in well-drained soil and allow the soil to dry out between waterings. Pull up and discard any affected plants at the first sign of attack. Avoid future problems by solarizing the soil (see page 150). Clean tools with rubbing alcohol after use.

Okra, a native to Africa, is actually a relative of the ornamental hibiscus. Both green and red varieties are available. Shown here: 'Louisiana Green Velvet'.

ONIONS
Allium cepa

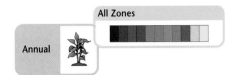

Annual — All Zones

All onions, including the variety 'Mars' shown here, need a rich, well-drained soil. During the early part of their growth, don't be shy with either water or fertilizer. But once they start forming bulbs, cut back on both water and fertilizer. Too much of either will result in double-bulbs and poor storage qualities.

Fusarium Basal Rot

Fusarium basal rot shows up with yellow tips on onion foliage, which may progress to rot at the soil line of the bulb, destroying the plant completely. When plants are dug, roots will be rotted. Dig up and destroy any affected plants at the first sign of attack. Grow certified disease-free plants. To avoid the problem, control onion maggots (see page 53), rotate onion plantings in different garden plots each year or grow in raised beds.

Several Italian onion varieties—including 'Florence Red', 'Rossa di Lucca' and 'Cipollini' (shown here), have recently been introduced to American gardens.

French knights returning from the Crusades are credited with introducing shallots to Europe. A type of multiplier onion, shallots have the habit of dividing into a clump of smaller bulbs that look like tiny tulip bulbs.

Shallots are a very satisfying crop to grow—especially if you like to cook. Shallots should return ten times the number of bulbs you planted.

Egyptian onions (Allium cepa) belong to a group known as Proliferum. As the name suggests, these types are prolific and multiply (like shallots), producing many bulblets from each mother bulb.

Purple Blotch

Purple blotch is a fungal disease that only affects onions, particularly during periods of warm, humid weather. It shows as damage on onion foliage, first appearing as white spots, quickly progressing to slick, purple blotches. If this disease has been a problem before, try planting onions in a different garden location, and provide generous spacing between plants for optimum air circulation.

Smut

Smut affects young onion sprouts, showing up as gray streaks in the foliage, and eventually producing a powdery mold. Avoid the problem by starting onions from sets or strong transplants.

Thrips

Thrips damage appears as silvery or brown spots or streaking on leaves and flowers. Control weeds around plants. Start by knocking thrips off with a strong blast of water. If thrips persist, use an insecticidal soap or azadirachtin (see pages 140 and 143).

Additional Pests:

Onion maggots and pink root will occasionally attack onions. Check the Quick Solution Chart on pages 36-61 for controls.

One 19th century gourmet summed up onions this way: "Without onions there would be no gastronomic art. Banish it from the kitchen and all pleasure of eating flies with it . . ." Shown here, the variety 'Copra'.

Onions are one of the world's oldest cultivated crops, used in cuisines virtually everywhere. Shown here are the varieties 'Mambo', 'Copper King' and 'Ailsa Craig Exhibition'.

OREGANO
Origanum vulgare

Perennial | Zones 5-9

Aphids

Aphids, those masses of small tan, green or black insects, sometimes congregate on the new growth of oregano. Start control by knocking aphids off with a strong blast of water. Attract beneficial insects by planting small-flowered nectar plants, such as dill, Queen-Anne's-lace and yarrow. If they persist, use an insecticidal soap or azadirachtin (see pages 140 and 143). Chemical controls include products that contain diazinon or malathion (see page 147).

Many plants sold as oregano are extremely ornamental, such as the golden-colored form of oregano, shown here. It is sold as oregano 'Aureum'.

Spider Mites

Spider mites often attack plants stressed by lack of water. Leaves will appear speckled, along with minute webbing; affected foliage will eventually turn yellow and drop. Avoid spider mites by keeping plants well watered. Control by spraying infested foliage with a strong blast of water. Attract beneficial insects by planting small-flowered nectar plants, such as dill, Queen-Anne's-lace and yarrow. If the problem persists, spray with insecticidal soap or light horticultural oil (see page 143).

It helps to know that the word "oregano" technically refers to a flavor rather than a group of plants. Many unrelated plants share the oregano flavor, which has resulted in a great deal of confusion for home gardeners. Shown here, the so-called "creeping oregano."

The flavor of oregano, such as the Italian oregano shown here, has long been associated with foods of the Mediterranean region—especially tomato-based dishes.

Greek oregano, pictured here, is technically Origanum vulgare *subsp.* hirtum, *but it may also be sold as* O. heracleoticum.

Fusarium Wilt

Fusarium wilt is a frustrating soil-borne disease that causes oregano plants to turn yellow or individual leaves to turn brown, eventually killing the plant. Avoid the problem by incorporating plenty of leaf mold or peat moss into the soil to improve soil drainage. If fusarium wilt attacks, completely remove and discard the affected plant, along with any soil the roots have come into contact with. If fusarium wilt has previously been a problem, plant oregano in another location. If practical, solarizing the soil (see page 150) will control soil-borne diseases.

Leaf Miners

Light brown trails in oregano leaves are the telltale marks of serpentine leaf miners—tiny larvae that burrow inside the leaves. Control by cutting off and discarding any affected foliage. Use floating rowcovers to exclude these pests (see page 145). Prevent future infestations with a soil application of beneficial nematodes (see page 149).

Oreganos are among those plants whose attributes make them equally at home in the flower border or vegetable garden. Shown here, is the highly ornamental (and flavorful) variety known as 'Herren Hausen'.

Variegated oregano makes a wonderful edging plant. It is perfect for spilling over rock walls or lining a sunny walk.

PARSLEY
Petroselinum crispum

Biennial

All Zones

Parsley is a biennial that will return to your garden the second year after it is planted. If it is allowed to go to seed, you may never have to plant parsley again; it readily self-sows .

develop into the even more beautiful black-and-yellow swallowtail butterfly, the best control is to cover parsley with a floating rowcover (see page 145), to keep pests from infesting the crop in the first place, handpick or simply plant extra parsley for these beautiful members of the butterfly family.

Root-Knot Nematodes

Characteristic nematode damage causes parsley to grow slowly, probably exhibiting wilted foliage even when adequate moisture is present in the soil. Either rotate your parsley plantings to a different part of the garden each year, or solarize the planting bed (see page 150) or add a significant amount of compost to help control the nematodes.

Carrot Rust Fly Larvae

If you notice retarded, pale growth with your parsley, and reddish tunnels on the roots, the problem can be traced to the larvae of the carrot rust fly. The best control is to cover carrots with a floating rowcover (see page 145), to keep pests from infesting the crop in the first place. Drench the affected plants with liquid seaweed at the base to help the plant shake off the attack.

Additional Pests:

Aphids, fusarium wilt, slugs and snails will occasionally attack parsley. Check the Quick Solution Chart on pages 36-61 for controls.

Parsley Worms

Missing or skeletonized parsley foliage indicates the presence of the 1- to 2-inch-long, white, green and black striped parsley worms, known for their menacing orange horns when aggravated. Because these beautiful worms

'Italian Broadleaf' parsley has large, flat leaves and is more intensely flavored than the curly-leafed types.

Parsley is native from Lebanon to Sardinia. Although it is largely used as a garnish in this country, its distinctive flavor is key to many national dishes throughout the Mediterranean and Near East.

PARSNIPS
Pastinaca sativa

Annual — All Zones

Parsnips require a fairly long growing period—from 100 to 120 days—and must be subjected to near freezing temperatures in the ground to change the root's natural starches to sugar; this results in the sweet, nutty flavor for which they are famous.

145), to keep pests from infesting the crop in the first place, handpick or simply plant extra parsley for these beautiful members of the butterfly family.

Canker and Leaf Spot

Canker and leaf spot is a fungal disease that attacks parsnips only, and particularly in the Northeast. It shows up as dark, sunken spots on the tops of parsnips. Avoid the problem by doing a thorough cleanup of all parsnip foliage and other debris in the fall, and by digging generous amounts of compost into the planting bed. If this disease has been a problem before, rotate parsnips to a different part of the garden.

Carrot Rust Fly Larvae

If you notice retarded, pale growth, and reddish tunnels on the parsnips themselves, the problem can be traced to the larvae of the carrot rust fly. The best control is to cover parsnips with a floating rowcover (see page 145), to keep pests from infesting the crop in the first place.

Parsley Worms

Missing or skeletonized parsnip foliage indicates the presence of the 1- to 2-inch-long, white, green and black striped parsley worms, known for their menacing orange horns when aggravated. Because these beautiful worms develop into the even more beautiful black-and-yellow swallowtail butterfly, the best control is to cover parsley with a floating rowcover (see page

For the largest and straightest roots, grow parsnips in a rich, deeply dug soil, or in raised beds filled with loam.

Left to overwinter in the ground, parsnips will likely flower the following spring. And for the record, according to the USDA, "there is no basis for the belief that parsnips that remain in the ground over winter are poisonous."

PEAS
Pisum sativum

Annual

All Zones

Mice or Birds

See pages 22-29 for control of these pests, which eat the peas right out of the soil, even before they have a chance to germinate.

Root Rot

If you notice the base of your pea plants rotting and turning black, the problem is root rot. Dig up and discard infected plants at the first sign of attack. Avoid the problem by planting peas in a very well-drained soil, amended with plenty of compost, leaf mold or peat moss.

Peas, such as the variety 'Stringless Snap', shown here, require a well-drained soil and some kind of trellis or fence on which to climb.

Mosaic Virus

Pea enation mosaic is a virus disease, usually spread by aphids. It appears as yellow blotches on the topsides of leaves, eventually forming blisters on the under-sides. There's no control, so best bet is to plant resistant varieties (see pages 19-21).

Pea Stunt

Pea stunt does just what the name says: stunts both pea flowers and foliage. This disease is spread by sap-sucking aphids, which can be controlled with a strong blast of water or with an application of insecticidal soap (see page 143). Encourage beneficial insects, such as lady beetles and lacewings (see pages 148-149).

Additional Pests:

Aphids, cutworms and powdery mildew will occasionally attack peas. Check the Quick Solution Chart on pages 36-61 for controls.

The variety known as 'Blue Pod' is known as one of the "soup peas."

Chinese or snow peas can be harvested when very young—really any time after the flower falls and the pods begin to form. For the best flavor, harvest when the pod has reached maximum size and the peas inside are just beginning to swell.

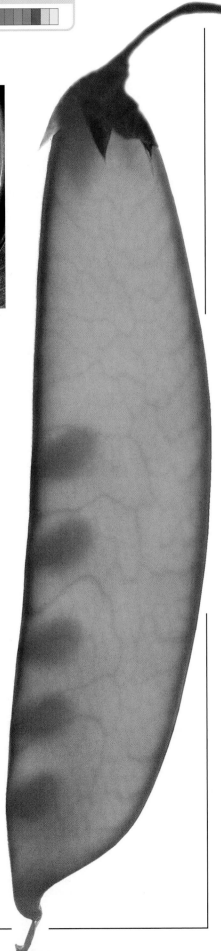

PEPPERS
Capsicum spp.

All Zones

Annual

It wasn't that long ago that about the only pepper grown in home gardens was the familiar green "bell" pepper. But today's gardeners have a veritable rainbow of choices.

Pepper Weevils

The pepper weevil is a very frustrating insect that causes almost mature peppers to fall from the plant, most commonly in southern and southwestern gardens. Encourage natural predators such as birds and wasps. Rotate crops.

Root-Knot Nematodes

Characteristic nematode damage causes peppers to grow slowly, probably exhibiting wilted foliage even when adequate moisture is present in the soil. Either rotate your peppers plantings to a different part of the garden each year, or solarize the planting bed (see page 150), or add significant amount of compost to help control the nematodes, or use an application of chitin (see page 141).

Ornamental 'Christmas' peppers.

'Merrimack Wonder' peppers.

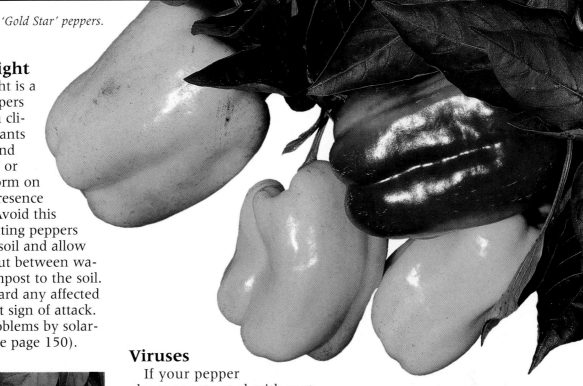

'Gold Star' peppers.

Southern Blight

Southern blight is a problem for peppers planted in warm climates. Whole plants rot at the base and strange webbing or fungus strings form on the soil in the presence of this disease. Avoid this problem by planting peppers in well-drained soil and allow the soil to dry out between waterings. Add compost to the soil. Pull up and discard any affected plants at the first sign of attack. Avoid future problems by solarizing the soil (see page 150).

'Ariane' peppers.

Viruses

If your pepper plants are stunted with mottled, streaked or unusually colored foliage, the problem is a virus. As there is no cure for virus diseases, dig up and destroy any infected plants at the first sign of attack. Help avoid virus diseases by controlling insects, such as aphids and leafhoppers, that spread viruses as they suck on plants.

A spray of insecticidal soap will control both aphids and leafhoppers (see page 143). Plant resistant varieties (see pages 19-21).

Additional Pests:

Bacterial spot, blister beetles, blossom-end rot, cutworms, damping off and tomato hornworms will occasionally attack peppers. Check the Quick Solution Chart on pages 36-61 for controls.

No vegetable has increased in popularity as quickly as the hot pepper. There are so many types—and so many different flavors and degrees of pungency—that it would take many gardening seasons to experience them all.

'Variegata' peppers.

POTATOES
Solanum tuberosum

Annual   All Zones

Potato Leafhoppers

Potato leafhoppers are small (approximately 1/8-inch-long), wedge-shaped insects which, true to their name, hop up from the leaves when disturbed. If not controlled early, potato leafhoppers will cause the edges of leaves to turn brown and curl. As they feed on the undersides of leaves, leafhoppers inject a toxic substance into the plant which, ultimately, may result in a greatly reduced potato yield. Leafhoppers may be controlled with insecticidal soap or light horticultural oil (see page 143). Chemical controls include insecticides containing carbaryl, malathion or pyrethrins (see page 147). When using any insecticide, pay special attention to the undersides of leaves where leafhoppers hide.

Potato Stalk Borers

Potato stalk borers and common stalk borers affect potatoes. Common stalk borers are brown, 3/4- to 1 1/2-long caterpillars that bore holes right in the stems of the plant and live inside, eating the plants from the inside out. If sections of plants suddenly wilt, despite sufficient water, check for telltale small holes in the stems surrounded by a fine sawdust-like material called frass. Dig up and destroy any infected plants, or portions of plants. These damaging caterpillars can be controlled with a spray of Bt (see page 141).

Native to the Andes, potatoes are available in a dizzying array of sizes, colors and shapes, many of which are considered "heirloom."

'Red Pontiac' potatoes.

'Frontier Russet' potatoes.

Aster Yellows

Aster yellows, a virus disease, occasionally attacks potatoes. Affected leaves will be weakened and have a mottled yellow appearance. As there is no cure for viral diseases, simply remove and destroy any affected plants. Wash hands with soap and hot water after touching foliage affected with aster yellows, as the virus can be spread by simply touching leaves and flowers of healthy plants. If you use pruning shears to cut out affected foliage, dip the blades in rubbing alcohol after use to disinfect.

Ring Spot

Ring spot is a bacterial disease that infects both the top portion of potatoes as well as the underground tubers. Foliage damage shows up as yellow, stunted leaves; when tubers are dug, they may be cracked with a dark ring of decay inside. Dig up and discard any infected tubers. After working with diseased plants, disinfect all tools used with rubbing alcohol. To avoid the problem next time, plant only certified disease-free seed potatoes.

'Yukon Gold' potatoes.

Additional Pests:

Colorado potato beetles, early blight, flea beetles, late blight, scab, slugs and wireworms will occasionally attack potatoes. Check the Quick Solution Chart on pages 36-61 for controls.

Diversity within the family: 'Yellow Finn', 'All Red' and 'Peruvian Purple' potatoes.

'Purple Viking' potatoes.

RADISHES
Raphanus sativus

Annual

All Zones

One of the sure signs of spring, radishes are usually the first harvest of the growing season. Radishes can be planted as soon as the ground is ready in early spring; they mature just a few weeks later.

Flea Beetles

Flea beetles cause radish foliage to be shot through with small holes or tan spots. When infected foliage is disturbed,

With their diminutive size, radishes are an ideal crop to grow in containers.

these tiny dark beetles jump just like fleas. May cause undersized radishes, especially if flea beetles attack when radish plants are small. Floating row-covers will exclude these pests (see page 145). An application of beneficial nematodes will keep them from harming future crops (see page 149). Smart gardeners avoid the problem altogether by planting radishes late in the growing season, after flea beetles have left the scene. Chemical controls include insecticides containing diazinon or pyrethrins (see page 147).

Fall Armyworms

Fall armyworms are dark caterpillars, approximately 1 inch long, that eat seedlings of radish plants at night, usually in late summer. For a small infestation, control by handpicking and disposing of these pests. Control with an application of Btk (see page 141).

Additional Pests:

Cabbage maggots will occasionally attack radishes. Check the Quick Solution Chart on pages 36-61 for controls.

RHUBARB
Rheum rhabarbarum

Zones 3-9

Perennial

Rhubarb Curculios

Rhubarb curculios cause plants to diminish in size and vigor. You'll have to look close to see the culprit: $1/2$-inch long grayish beetles with snouts used to bore into rhubarb stalks. To avoid rhubarb curculios, remove their favorite host plants—sunflowers, thistle and curly dock.

Southern Blight

Southern blight is a problem for rhubarb planted in warm climates. Whole plants rot at the base and strange webbing or fungus strings form on the soil in the presence of this disease. Avoid this problem by planting rhubarb in well-drained soil and allow the soil to dry out between waterings. Pull up and discard any affected plants and soil at the first sign of attack. Avoid future problems by solarizing the soil (see page 150) and rotating crops.

Along with asparagus and artichokes, rhubarb is one of the few perennials grown in vegetable gardens. Three or four plants will be enough for the average household. Rhubarb returns year after year with its delightful spring crop of pinkish-red stems.

Old-timers called rhubarb the "pie plant" for good reason: For many, there's no better pie than a rhubarb pie.

Phytophthora Crown Rot

Phytophthora crown rot causes leaves to wilt and makes brown sunken spots of decay at the base of rhubarb stalks. Severe infections may cause whole plants to collapse. Remove and destroy any infected plants. Avoid the problem by planting rhubarb in well-drained soil, and don't overwater plants. If crown rot has been a problem in the past, spray rhubarb with a Bordeaux mixture, copper sulfate or a fungicide containing captan before the disease can attack (see pages 141-146).

Additional Pests:

Fusarium wilt, Japanese beetles and verticillium wilt will occasionally attack rhubarb. Check the Quick Solution Chart on pages 36-61 for controls.

ROSEMARY
Rosmarinus officinalis

Zones 8-10

Woody Perennial

Black Scale

Scale-infested rosemary plants will have waxy bumps on stems. The tough outer coating on scale protects the small insects inside, which do damage by sucking plant juices from the stems. If left untreated, the scale will eventually produce a sticky, honeydew secretion that attracts ants and a blackish mildew. If the infestation is not large, simply scrape the scale off the plant using the edge of a dull knife or a plastic scouring pad. Avoid problems with scale by attracting such natural predators as lacewing larvae and beneficial wasps (see page 149) or by growing small-flowered nectar plants, such as scabiosa, yarrow and dill.

Mealybugs

You'll definitely know if your rosemary has mealybugs: their distinctive fuzzy white bodies (about $1/4$ inch long) look like nothing else in the pest world. If you notice mealybugs on the foliage, start control by knocking them off with a strong blast of water. Attract beneficial insects by planting small-flowered nectar plants, such as scabiosa, dill and yarrow. Dab individual mealybugs with a cotton swab dipped in alcohol. If the infestation continues, spray with an insecticidal soap, paying special attention to the undersides of leaves (see page 143). Chemical controls include products containing malathion, carbaryl or diazinon (see pages 146-147).

'Tuscan Blue' rosemary, with rosemary's customary blue blossoms. Other varieties are available with dark blue, pink or white flowers.

Native to the Mediterranean, rosemary is used to difficult conditions: lean, very fast-draining soil, little in the way of nutrients and very little water during the growing season. For the best results, try to mimic those conditions in your own garden. One thing is for certain: Rosemary will not tolerate wet feet!

Cooks know that a little bit of rosemary tends to go a long way. Its refreshing, resinous, piney, sweet scent is like none other, but it is so distinctive that, if used with too free a hand, it will overwhelm other flavors in the dish.

Whiteflies

If your rosemary plants are lacking in vigor, pale, and clouds of very small white insects fly up when the leaves are disturbed, you've got an infestation of whiteflies. To control, either use an insecticidal soap (see page 143), or simply blast the whiteflies off the plants with a strong spray of water. Yellow sticky traps can be effective (see page 145). Attract beneficial insects by planting small-flowered nectar plants, such as yarrow and dill.

In areas with mild winter climates, rosemary plants can achieve great size. Depending on the type, rosemary will either cascade over garden walls or grow upright to four feet or more.

In cold winter climates you can transplant garden-grown rosemary into a pot and bring it indoors for the winter. Give rosemary the brightest window available and let it dry out between waterings.

Gray Mold

Botrytis blight is also known as gray mold. Symptoms of this disease include drooping flowers that then turn brown and become covered with a gray, fuzzy mold. Dig up and destroy any infected plants at the first sign of attack. Mulch to avoid having the mud splash on the rosemary leaves. Avoid the problem by avoiding overhead watering, making sure the soil has excellent drainage and by spacing plants far apart to improve air circulation. Existing disease cannot be cured, but future outbreaks can be prevented with a fungicide containing chlorothalonil (see page 146).

Additional Pests:

Aphids, fusarium wilt and spider mites will occasionally attack rosemary. Check the Quick Solution Chart on pages 36-61 for controls.

RUE
Ruta graveolens

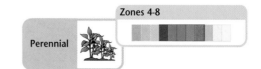

Perennial   Zones 4-8

Rue produces aromatic, fernlike foliage on plants two to three feet tall. Use caution when cutting branches, as sap from rue causes skin irritation in some people.

Whiteflies

If your rue plants are lacking in vigor, pale, and clouds of very small white insects fly up when the leaves are disturbed, you've got an infestation of whiteflies. To control, either use an insecticidal soap (see page 143), or simply blast the whiteflies off the plants with a strong spray of water. Yellow sticky traps can be effective (see page 145). Attract beneficial insects by planting small-flowered nectar plants, such as yarrow and dill.

Parsley Worms

Rue foliage shot with holes or with ragged edges probably indicates the presence of these 1- to 2-inch-long, white, green and black striped parsley worms, known for their menacing orange horns when aggravated. Because these beautiful worms develop into the even more beautiful black-and-yellow swallowtail butterfly, the best control is to cover rue with a floating rowcover (see page 145), to keep pests from infesting the crop in the first place, handpick or simply plant extra parsley for these beautiful members of the butterfly family.

RUTABAGAS
Brassica napus,
Napobrassica **group**

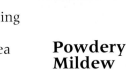

Aphids

Aphids, those masses of small tan, green or black insects, sometimes congregate on the new growth of rutabaga. Start control by knocking aphids off with a strong blast of water. Attract beneficial insects such as lady beetles and lacewings by planting small-flowered nectar plants, such as dill, Queen-Anne's-lace and yarrow. If they persist, use an insecticidal soap or azadirachtin (see pages 140 and 143). Chemical controls include products that contain diazinon or malathion.

Flea Beetles

Flea beetles cause rutabaga foliage to be shot through with small holes or tan spots. When infected foliage is disturbed, these tiny dark beetles jump just like fleas. May cause undersized rutabagas, especially if flea beetles attack when rutabaga plants are small. Floating rowcovers will exclude these pests (see page 145). An application of beneficial nematodes will keep them from harming future crops (see page 149). Spray plants with an insecticidal soap (see page 143). Smart gardeners avoid the problem altogether by planting rutabagas late in the growing season, after flea beetles have left the scene. Chemical controls include insecticides containing diazinon or pyrethrins (see page 147).

Rutabagas take a relatively long time to mature—around 100 days—and like other members of the cabbage family, prefer cool growing conditions. These traits combine to make them tough to grow outside northern areas of the country, where summer temperatures average around 75°F.

Rutabagas are thought to be a naturally occurring hybrid between a turnip and a cabbage. This phenomenon probably occurred as recently as the Middle Ages.

Powdery Mildew

Powdery mildew may become a problem during periods of humid weather. Although the disease is not fatal, its signature powdery white coating on foliage and flowers is unattractive. Remove and destroy any infected plants. Prevent further outbreaks of powdery mildew with a baking soda spray (see page 141). Rotate crops.

Additional Pests:

Cabbage maggots will occasionally attack rutabaga. Check the Quick Solution Chart on pages 36-61 for controls.

Sage
Salvia officinalis

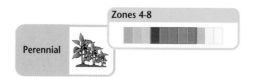

Perennial

Zones 4-8

Bacterial Wilt

If your sage suddenly wilts, even though there's sufficient moisture in the soil, bacterial wilt is the probable cause—especially if there's been an extended period of warm weather. Dig up and destroy any infected plants at the first sign of attack. Remove all soil the roots have touched. Use floating rowcovers (see page 145). Avoid problems in the future by incorporating plenty of organic matter into the planting beds, and keep them free of garden debris. Maximize air circulation by not overcrowding plants.

Fusarium Wilt

Fusarium wilt is a frustrating soil-borne disease that causes sage plants to turn yellow, or individual leaves to turn brown, eventually killing the plant. Avoid the problem by incorporating plenty of leaf mold or peat moss into the soil to improve soil drainage. If fusarium wilt attacks, completely remove and discard the affected plant, along with any soil the roots have come into contact with. If fusarium wilt has previously been a problem, plant sage in another location.

Sage is known to cooks as the herb that makes any poultry stuffing what it should be. It is also an essential flavor ingredient in sausages and meat loaves.

A collection of sages: Salvia officinalis, *'Purpurascens' and 'Berggarten'.*

For beautiful yellow-and-green varie-gated leaves, plant either 'Icterina', shown here, or the variety called 'Aurea'.

Purple-leafed sages, such as the 'Purpurascens' variety shown here, are beautiful additions to the herb or flower garden. But they are not as hardy, or as flavorful as other sages.

Spider Mites

Spider mites can attack sage, especially during periods of hot, dry weather. Telltale damage includes stippled, grayish foliage and stunted growth. They attack the undersides of leaves and usually leave small holes and fine webbing in their wake. Blast mites off with a strong spray of water, paying particular attention to the undersides of the leaves. Attract beneficial insects by planting small-flowered nectar plants, such as dill, Queen-Anne's-lace and yarrow. If the problem persists, use an insecticidal soap (see page 143) specially formulated for the control of mites.

Slugs and Snails

If you wake up in the morning and find that something has eaten major portions of your sage new growth and you spot telltale slime trails—you'll know the culprits are slugs and/or snails. Edge plants in copper strips (see page 142). Place saucers of beer around the plants to create traps. Although there are a number of more or less effective natural controls, even the most ardent organic gardeners have begun using a product called Escar-Go, which contains iron phosphate, a naturally occurring soil element (see page 144), to control these frustrating pests. Chemical controls include products (usually in bait form) containing metaldehyde or methiocarb (see page 147). Whether using Escar-Go or a chemical control, scatter it all around potential targets and any damp, shady spot where slugs and snails hide during the day. If you know there are slugs and/or snails in your area, always treat your garden with a control before their damage is apparent; slugs and snails can do a tremendous amount of damage in even one night.

Sages are among the most beautiful of all herbs, taking their place proudly in the flower or shrub border. The variety 'Berggarten' has extra-large, gray-green leaves; 'Icterina' is variegated, yellow and green.

SALAD BURNET
Sanguisorba minor

Perennial   Zones 3-8

Fusarium Wilt

Fusarium wilt is a frustrating soil-borne disease that causes salad burnet plants to turn yellow, or individual leaves to turn brown, eventually killing the plant. Avoid the problem by incorporating plenty of leaf mold or peat moss into the soil to improve soil drainage. If fusarium wilt attacks, completely remove and discard the affected plant, along with any soil the roots have come into contact with. If fusarium wilt has previously been a problem, plant salad burnet in another location.

Salad burnet is a highly underutilized herb. It makes a nice-looking, tidy plant with finely cut foliage. In the kitchen the leaves, flowers and seeds of salad burnet are valued for their delicate cucumber flavor—an excellent addition to any salad.

SPINACH
Spinacia oleracea

Annual   All Zones

Spinach Leaf Miners

Pale tunnels winding their way through spinach leaves indicate the presence of leaf miners. Remove and discard any infected leaves at the first sign of attack. Avoid the problem by using floating rowcovers. If the problem persists, spray weekly with an insecticide containing diazinon or malathion (see page 147).

Spinach varieties are divided between two types: smooth-leaved and savoy, which have puckered and folded leaves. While both have a similar flavor, savoy types have a little denser texture while smooth-leaved types are very tender, especially when picked young.

Green Peach Aphids

Aphids, those masses of small, pale green insects, sometimes congregate on the undersides of spinach leaves. Start control by knocking aphids off with a strong blast of water. If they persist, spray weekly with an insecticidal soap (see page 143).

Spinach Flea Beetles

Spinach flea beetles cause spinach foliage to be shot through with small holes or tan spots. When infected foliage is disturbed, these tiny dark beetles jump just like fleas. Floating rowcovers will exclude these pests (see page 145). Smart gardeners avoid the problem altogether by planting spinach late in the growing season, after flea beetles have left the scene. Use white sticky traps (see page 145).

Spinach Blight

Spinach blight is a disease that causes stunted spinach leaves, sometimes with yellow or brownish edges, or a wrinkled appearance. There is no effective control; avoid the problem altogether by planting resistant varieties of spinach (see pages 19-21). Remove and destroy diseased plants at the first sign of attack. Be sure to control weeds around the plants.

Blue Mold

Blue mold keeps the spinach crop from maturing, showing up as blue spots on immature, fallen foliage or yellow tips. Although there is no control, avoid the problem by rotating spinach plantings in different garden plots each year and by planting resistant varieties (see

Spinach planted in early August will often produce a sizeable crop before the first frost or snow arrives.

pages 19-21). Some help is provided by planting spinach in a full-sun location, with wide spacing between plants to encourage maximum air circulation and control weeds around the plants.

Additional Pests:

Slugs will occasionally attack spinach. Check the Quick Solution Chart on pages 36-61 for controls.

Spinach demands a rich, moist, well-drained soil to succeed. It performs best during cool weather.

SUMMER SQUASH
Cucurbita pepo

All Zones

Annual

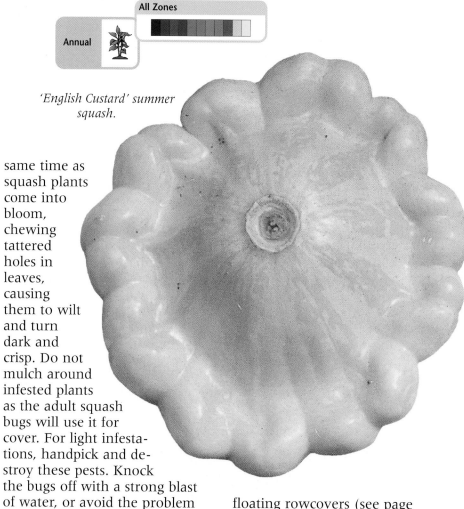

'English Custard' summer squash.

Squash Vine Borer

The damage from these 1-inch-long, white worms, which actually bore right into squash stems, shows up with wilted foliage. There's not much the gardener can do once the worm has entered the protection of the stem. You can either prune away the affected part of the plant, or make a slit in the stem where you notice a sawdust-like material (called frass), and remove the worm, taping the stem back together again. Avoid the problem altogether by using floating rowcovers (see page 145) to keep the adult moths from laying eggs on the squash plants.

Squash Bugs

Squash bugs are grayish-brown bugs with orange markings, approximately 3/4 inch long. They show up about the same time as squash plants come into bloom, chewing tattered holes in leaves, causing them to wilt and turn dark and crisp. Do not mulch around infested plants as the adult squash bugs will use it for cover. For light infestations, handpick and destroy these pests. Knock the bugs off with a strong blast of water, or avoid the problem in the first place with the use of floating rowcovers (see page 145) or by planting resistant squash varieties (see pages 19-21). If infestation continues, control with an insecticidal soap (see page 143). Chemical controls include insecticides containing carbaryl or pyrethrins (see pages 146-147).

'Storr's Green' zucchini.

'Early Prolific Straightneck' summer squash.

'Zephyr' summer squash.

'Golden Bush' summer squash.

Viruses

If your summer squash are stunted with mottled, streaked or unusually colored foliage, the problem is a virus. As there is no cure for virus diseases, dig up and destroy any infected plants at the first sign of attack. Help avoid virus diseases by controlling in-sects such as aphids and leafhoppers, which spread viruses as they suck on plants. A spray of insecticidal soap will control both aphids and leafhoppers (see page 143).

Additional Pests:

Slugs will occasionally attack summer squash. Check the Quick Solution Chart on pages 36-61 for controls.

Choanephora Wet Rot

Choanephora wet rot causes immature squash to shrivel and turn black on one end. Most likely to be a problem during periods of damp, warm weather, this disease will often disappear on its own with the return of dry weather. Other than planting squash far enough apart to promote good air circulation, there are no controls.

'Golden Scallop' summer squash.

'Ronde de Nice' summer squash.

SWEET POTATOES
Ipomoea batatas

Annual

All Zones

There are two basic types of sweet potatoes: one with a mealy, yellowish flesh, and the other with moister, sweeter, orange to red-orange flesh.

Sweet Potato Flea Beetles

Sweet potato flea beetles cause sweet potato foliage to be shot through with small holes or tan spots. When infected foliage is disturbed, these tiny dark beetles jump just like fleas. Destroy host weeds such as bindweed and wild morning glory, which these pests also feed on. Smart gardeners avoid the problem altogether by using floating rowcovers (see page 145). Avoid the problem in the future with an application of beneficial nematodes (see page 149).

Sweet potatoes have long been grown in this country, particularly in the South, while yams are rarely grown outside the tropics.

Summer's over: A harvest of sweet potatoes and squash.

so wise gardeners avoid the problem by only planting certified disease-free slips. Remove and discard any infected plants at the first sign of attack and disinfect any tools used with rubbing alcohol.

Root-Knot Nematodes

Characteristic nematode damage causes sweet potatoes to grow slowly, probably exhibiting wilted foliage even when adequate moisture is present in the soil. Either rotate your sweet potato plantings to a different part of the garden each year, or solarize the planting bed (see page 150), or add significant amount of compost to help control the nematodes or use an application of chitin (see page 141).

Sweet Potato Weevils

Sweet potato weevils are considered the worst insect pest of sweet potatoes. Harvested tubers will be tunneled through with small, deep holes. Best bet is to begin with certified beetle-free transplants and to remove any wild morning glory that may be in the vicinity, as it is a host plant for this pesky insect. Remove and destroy any infected plants.

Black Rot

Black rot is a disease that appears as dark, sunken spots on sweet potato tubers, yellowish stunted foliage and possibly dark lesions on the stems right at soil level. There is no control,

Additional Pests:

Fusarium wilt will occasionally attack sweet potato. Check the Quick Solution Chart on pages 36-61 for controls.

Good gardeners and cooks know that sweet potatoes and yams are not the same thing: Sweet potatoes belong to the genus Ipomoea *and yams to the genus* Dioscorea.

SWISS CHARD
Beta vulgaris,
Cicla group

Annual

All Zones

Spinach Leaf Miners

The damage from these minute pests—the larvae of a fly—shows up as light tan serpentine lines on swiss chard leaves. For a light infestation, handpick these pests and destroy them. Hard to control once the pests have mined their way into the leaves, best bet is to avoid the problem in the first place with the use of floating rowcovers (see page 145).

Tarnished Plant Bugs

Tarnished plant bugs are most active in the early spring but may persist through summer. As they feed on foliage, they inject toxins into the plant, which results in deformed foliage that may eventually turn black. For light infestation, handpick and destroy these bugs. Use floating rowcovers to exclude these pests (see page 145). Control tarnished plant bugs with a spray of insecticidal soap (see page 143).

Cercospora Leaf Spot

Different-sized spots on swiss chard leaves, in shades of brown, black, purple or yellow are a sure sign of leaf spot. Best bet is to completely remove and destroy any affected plants at the first sign of attack. Avoid the problem by watering plants early in the day to allow foliage to dry before evening, and avoid wetting the foliage. If you use pruning shears to remove diseased foliage, dip the blades in rubbing alcohol before reuse. Rotate crops.

Additional Pests:

Flea beetles and grasshoppers will occasionally attack swiss chard. Check the Quick Solution Chart on pages 36-61 for controls.

'Silverado Compact' Swiss chard.

'Bright Lights' Swiss chard. Although few people are aware of it, Swiss chard is a special variety of the common beet.

TARRAGON
Artemisia dracunculus var. *sativa*

Zones 4-7

Perennial

A pleasant combination of petunias and the true French tarragon, Artemisia dracunculus *var. 'Sativa'.*

Oregon Swallowtail Larvae

Oregon swallowtail larvae eat the edges of tarragon leaves, causing a ragged appearance. Because these caterpillars turn into swallowtail butterflies, most gardeners tolerate the damage or simply plant extra tarragon to feed the larvae for the short period of time they are present in the garden.

Fusarium Wilt

Fusarium wilt is a frustrating soil-borne disease which causes tarragon plants to turn yellow, or individual leaves to turn brown, eventually killing the plant. Avoid the problem by incorporating plenty of leaf mold or peat moss into the soil to improve soil drainage. If fusarium wilt attacks, completely remove and discard the affected plant, along with any soil the roots have come into contact with. If fusarium wilt has previously been a problem, plant tarragon in another location.

Powdery Mildew

Tarragon will occasionally be bothered by powdery mildew if growing conditions turn humid. Although the disease is not fatal, its signature powdery white coating on foliage and flowers is unattractive. Remove and destroy any infected plants. Prevent further outbreaks of powdery mildew with a baking soda spray (see page 141).

If you want that true, anise-like flavor associated with tarragon, make sure you buy the true French tarragon, not the Russian tarragon, Artemisia dracunculus dracunculoides.

THYME
Thymus spp.

Perennial

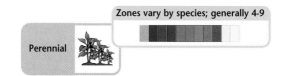

Zones vary by species; generally 4-9

Thymus vulgaris, the common thyme.

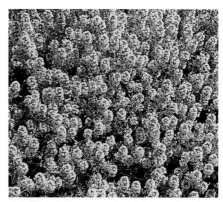

Woolly thyme.

Spider Mites

Spider mites can attack thyme, especially during periods of hot, dry weather. Telltale damage includes stippled, grayish foliage and stunted growth. They attack the undersides of leaves and usually leave small holes and fine webbing in their wake. Blast mites off with a strong spray of water, paying particular attention to the undersides of the leaves. Plant small-flowered nectar plants, such as yarrow and Queen-Anne's-lace to attract beneficial insects. If the problem persists, use an insecticidal soap (see page 143) specially formulated for the control of mites.

Fusarium Wilt

Fusarium wilt is a frustrating soil-borne disease that causes thyme plants to turn yellow, or individual leaves to turn brown, eventually killing the plant. Avoid the problem by incorporating plenty of leaf mold or peat moss into the soil to improve soil drainage. If fusarium wilt attacks, completely remove and discard the affected plant, along with any soil the roots have come into contact with. If fusarium wilt has previously been a problem, plant thyme in another location.

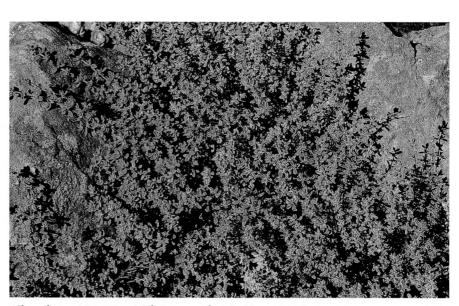

'Annie Hall' thyme.

*Silver thyme 'Argenteus' (*Thymus vulgaris *'Argenteus').*

TOMATOES
Lycopersicon esculentum

Annual | All Zones

A harvest of heirloom tomatoes.

'Great White' tomatoes.

Septoria Leaf Spot

Septoria leaf spot is a fungal disease that affects only tomato plants. It causes gray spots to form on tomato foliage, often with darker colored edges. Remove and destroy any infected leaves at the first sign of attack and avoid the spreading the problem by not wetting the foliage when watering the vines.

Tomato Fruitworms

Tomato fruitworms are the caterpillars of any number of moths; all feed on tomato fruit, causing scraped holes, usually at the top shoulders of the fruit. Caterpillars may be green, pink or brown. Begin control by simply handpicking theses large caterpillars; if infestation persists, spray with Btk (see page 141).

'Big Boy' tomato.

Root-Knot Nematodes

Characteristic nematode damage causes tomatoes to grow slowly, probably exhibiting wilted foliage even when adequate moisture is present in the soil. Either rotate your tomato plantings to a different part of the garden each year, or solarize the planting bed (see page 150) or add significant amount of compost to help control the nematodes, or use an application of chitin (see page 141). Best bet is to plant resistant varieties (see pages 19-21).

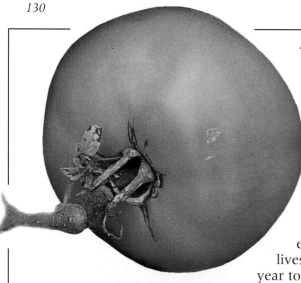

'Persimmon' tomato.

A variety of cherry tomatoes—the favored tomato for drying in Italy.

Verticillium Wilt

Verticillium wilt will cause tomato foliage to turn yellow with brown blotches. Portions of the plant may wilt suddenly. A fungus disease, verticillium wilt lives in garden soil from one year to the next. Space plants widely to improve air circulation. If it's been a problem before, try planting tomatoes in a different garden location. At the first sign of attack, make an application of liquid fertilizer; the resulting boost in growth may keep the plants from succumbing to the disease. Avoid the problem by planting tomato varieties resistant to this malady (see pages 19-21).

'San Marzano' paste tomatoes.

Tobacco Mosaic Virus

Tobacco mosaic virus causes tomato foliage to have a mottled appearance, usually dark green, brownish or yellow spots. As a virus, there are no cures; pull up and destroy any infected plants and disinfect any tools used with rubbing alcohol. Avoid the problem by planting tomato varieties resistant to this malady (see pages 19-21).

'Black Krim' tomatoes.

Additional Pests:

Anthracnose, aphids, bacterial wilt, blister beetles, blossom-end rot, early blight, flea beetles, fusarium wilt, late blight, tomato hornworms and spider mites will occasionally attack tomatoes. Check the Quick Solution Chart on pages 36-61 for controls.

'Green Zebra' tomatoes.

'Rainbow' stuffing tomatoes.

TURNIP
Brassica rapa,
Rapifera group

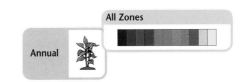

Annual | All Zones

One of the oldest cultivated vegetables—known to have been grown for over 4000 years—turnips are prized for both their swollen roots and leafy tops, and are favorites of fine cooks.

Powdery Mildew

Turnip will occasionally be bothered by powdery mildew if growing conditions turn humid. Although the disease is not fatal, its signature powdery white coating on foliage is unattractive. Remove and destroy any infected plants. Space plants widely to improve air circulation. Rotate crops. Prevent further outbreaks of powdery mildew with a baking soda spray (see page 141).

Additional Pests:

Cabbage maggots will occasionally attack turnips. Check the Quick Solution Chart on pages 36-61 for controls.

Flea Beetles

Flea beetles cause turnip foliage to be shot through with small holes or tan spots. When infected foliage is disturbed, these tiny dark beetles jump just like fleas. Floating rowcovers will exclude these pests (see page 145). If you don't use floating rowcovers, a spray of insecticidal soap will control flea beetles (see page 143). Smart gardeners avoid the problem altogether by planting turnips late in the growing season, after flea beetles have left the scene.

Aphids

Aphids, those masses of small tan, green or black insects, sometimes congregate on the new growth of turnip. Start control by knocking aphids off with a strong blast of water. Attract beneficial insects such as lady beetle and lacewing by planting small-flowered nectar plants, such as yarrow, dill or Queen-Anne's-lace. If they persist, use an insecticidal soap or azadirachtin (see pages 140 and 143). Chemical controls include products that contain diazinon or malathion.

WATERMELON
Citrullus lanatus

Annual — All Zones

'Orangelo' watermelon.

Birds
See pages 22-29 for control of these pests, which eat the watermelon seeds right out of the soil, even before they have a chance to germinate.

Cucumber Beetles
Spotted cucumber beetles munch on watermelon leaves, leaving holes or ragged edges. The beetles themselves are about 1/4 inch long, yellowish green in color, with black spots. For light infes-

'Georgia Rattlesnake' watermelon.

tations, handpick and destroy these pests. Use floating row-covers to exclude this pest. Plant resistant varieties. Beneficial nematodes will help prevent spotted cucumber beetles (see page 149). Chemical controls include products that contain carbaryl, diazinon or pyrethrins (see pages 146-147).

Gummy Stem Blight
Gummy stem blight is a fungus disease that causes leaves to turn prematurely yellow, often with gray spots. There is no control for this disease. Pull and destroy any infected plants at the first sign of attack. Avoid the problem by not planting watermelons in the same location where gummy stem blight has previously been a problem and do not use seeds saved from infected melons.

'Deuce of Hearts' seedless watermelon.

'Moon and Stars' heirloom watermelon.

You can't judge a watermelon by its rind!

Watermelon Fruit Blotch

Watermelon fruit blotch is a disease that causes brown sunken spots on the melons; if conditions are conducive, watermelon fruit blotch can wipe out an entire melon crop in a short period of time. Remove and destroy infected plants at the first sign of attack. Because this disease can be spread by water, avoid wetting the foliage of watermelon plants, soaking plants from the base instead. A spray of copper will prevent future outbreaks of this disease (see page 142).

Additional Pests:

Aphids, anthracnose, bacterial wilt, blister beetles, blossom-end rot, early blight, flea beetles, fusarium wilt, late blight, spider mite and tomato hornworms will occasionally attack watermelon. Check the Quick Solution Chart on pages 36-61 for controls.

Cercospora Leaf Spot

Different-sized spots on watermelon leaves, in shades of brown, black, purple or yellow, are a sure sign of leaf spot. Best bet is to completely remove and destroy any affected plants at the first sign of attack. Avoid the problem by watering plants early in the day to allow foliage to dry before evening, and avoid wetting the foliage. If you use pruning shears to remove diseased foliage, dip the blades in rubbing alcohol before reuse. Rotate crops.

'Sweet Siberian'—a Russian watermelon variety.

WINTER SQUASH AND PUMPKINS
Cucurbita maxima, C. mixta, C. moschata, and C. pepo var. pepo

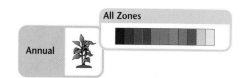

All Zones

Annual

'Maryland Pie' pumpkins.

'Emerald Bush Buttercup' winter squash.

Squash Bugs

Squash bugs are predominately brown or black, with a hint of their orange-colored body showing from under their wings. These relatives of the stink bug are approximately $1/2$ inch long and suck plant juices from leaves and vines, causing yellow spots that eventually turn brown. If infestation is allowed to persist, entire plants may turn brown and die, and fruit may be damaged, as well. Use floating row-covers to exclude this pest. For light infestation, handpick and destroy these pests.

Control squash bugs with a spray of insecticidal soap (see page 143). Chemical controls include insecticides containing rotenone, carbaryl and malathion (see pages 144-147).

Spaghetti squash.

'Mardi Gras' winter squash.

Cucumber Beetles

Striped (or spotted) cucumber beetles are small ($1/4$- to $1/3$-inch-long) beetles that don't do much damage initially, but may transmit bacterial wilt—a fatal disease for squash and pumpkin. First sign of attack from these beetles shows up with irregular holes chewed in leaves. Begin control by handpicking and destroying beetles. If infestation persists, spray with insecticide containing pyrethrum, diazinon or carbaryl (see pages 146-147). Spotted cucumber beetles munch on winter squash and pumpkin leaves, leaving holes or ragged edges. The beetles themselves are about $1/4$ inch long, yellowish green in color, with black spots. For light infestations, handpick and destroy these pests. Use floating rowcovers to exclude them. Beneficial nematodes will help prevent spotted cucumber beetles (see page 149). Chemical controls include products that contain carbaryl, diazinon or pyrethrins (see pages 146-147).

'Delicata' and 'Waltham Butternut' winter squash.

'Table King' compact winter squash.

Additional Pests:

Bacterial wilt and powdery mildew will occasionally attack winter squash and pumpkin. Check the Quick Solution Chart on pages 36-61 for controls.

'Washington Arikara' winter squash.

With their hard, shell-like skins and dense, moist flesh, winter squash make excellent "keepers." Squash often lasts throughout the entire winter if stored in a cool, dry place.

« CHAPTER 4 »
PREVENTION GLOSSARY

This section contains descriptions of dozens of garden care products designed to control or counteract the effects of vegetable pests. You don't need to stock them all, and you probably will use them only once you've tried some of the more environmentally friendly solutions listed. Get to know your own level of comfort with these products' effects, and use only the ones that you're confident of. You'll also find reminders about the safe handling of pesticides, because you'll sometimes be dealing with strong, occasionally deadly stuff! Remember that all these products have specific dosages. Don't fall into the mentality of "if a little works, a lot will work a lot better or quicker." It just isn't true, and remember, it's actually illegal to overdo recommended dosages. We can't repeat it enough: Always read the label and follow directions to the letter, and store any substance safely out of the reach of children and pets.

MEANS OF PREVENTION

It's not only a good idea, it's the law: Anyone using pesticides must read and follow all label instructions to the letter, including, when advised, the wearing of protective gear.

HOW TOXIC IS IT?

The relative toxicity of any pesticide is indicated on the product label with one of the following words, usually in large print.

Danger = Highly toxic

Poison = Highly toxic

Warning = Moderately toxic

Caution = Slightly toxic

If the product is relatively nontoxic, no word will appear on the label.

Throughout this book, we have ordered the solutions to your garden's pest problems from the most benign—in terms of toxicity to the environment—to the most extreme measures. In almost all cases, we think you'll find the least toxic solutions will work just fine, especially if you've followed the basics for a healthy garden, as outlined on pages 10-21. On these pages you'll find descriptions of the various products recommended throughout this book. They are intended for general information only: in every case where you use a commercially available pesticide, it's your responsibility—to yourself, your family, your pets and the environment—to read and follow all label instructions to the letter. This includes recommended dilution rates, application instructions and disposal instructions.

Disposal of leftover chemical pesticides represents a problem to most home gardeners—so much so that many communities have instituted special days during the year where one can bring hazardous materials to designated locations for safe disposal. Before, many people simply poured leftover pesticides down the drain, where these extremely concentrated poisons eventually found their way into rivers, streams and

There are many, many lessons to be learned from a garden, including the concept of being a responsible steward for a small piece of our planet.

WHAT'S IN A NAME?

The following terms are used frequently in conjunction with pest control. It will help you get the product you need if you know what to ask for.

Pesticide: An agent that kills pests (generally considered to include insects, mites, slugs and snails, nematodes and diseases).

Insecticide: An agent that kills insects.

Miticide: An agent that kills mites.

Molluscicide: An agent that kills slugs and snails.

Nematicide: An agent that kills nematodes.

Fungicide: An agent that kills fungus.

Herbicide: An agent that kills herbaceous plants (generally considered a "weed killer").

When you think of the intimate relationship most small children and toddlers have with their gardens, you think twice about what products you choose to control pests.

---

aquifers. If a pest situation is severe enough to require a chemical solution, instead of buying pesticides in concentrated forms (which very few gardeners are ever able to use completely), consider buying these products in a premixed (prediluted) form. Premixed pesticides are easier to use and sold in quantities most gardeners find easy to use up—a reasonable solution to the disposal problem.

TIP WHERE TO GET ANSWERS

If you have any questions about a pesticide you are using or are planning to use, check the telephone book for the state pesticide agency or the local office of the Environmental Protection Agency (EPA). The EPA and Texas Tech University Health Sciences Center School of Medicine have combined forces and set up the National Pesticide Telecommunications Network, a 24-hour telephone hotline that can be reached at 800-858-PEST.

Spray Safely

No matter what type of pesticide you use, there are certain rules you must follow for safety's sake.

Your Own Safety

Read the label every time you spray or dust, and note especially all the cautions and warnings. Mix sprays on a solid, level surface to avoid spillage. Avoid spilling pesticides on the skin or clothing, and wash exposed skin areas thoroughly with soap and water. Do not eat or smoke while spraying. Wash hands thoroughly with soap and water immediately

It's surprising how well the simple means of prevention work—like removing aphids by hand or with a blast of water from a garden hose. The trick is to catch infestations before they get out of control.

after spraying. Keep all chemicals out of the reach of pets and children. Store in a locked cabinet or on a high shelf. Set aside a special set of mixing tools, measuring spoons and a graduated measuring cup. Use them for mixing and measuring chemicals only. Be sure to keep all chemicals in their original labeled containers at all times. Follow all label instructions for disposing of leftover spray. Unused pesticides must be disposed of properly to avoid harming the environment. Check your community's hazardous materials department for their guidelines.

Natural Pesticides and Fungicides

When it comes time to choose a product for the control of a specific pest or disease, always start with the most environmentally benign one first. More times than not, it will control the problem handily.

In the past generation, a great number of products have come onto the market that are seen as an alternative to synthetic pesticides and fungicides. In general, this has been a good trend, resulting in more environmental consciousness on the part of home gardeners and less spraying of truly harmful products. One popular misconception persists, however: namely, that if a pesticide or fungicide is natural, it is safe. Granted, there are many natural pesticides that are not poisonous, but if the natural product is, in fact, a poison (such as pyrethrins derived from the chrysanthemum plant), it is just as poisonous as a synthetically produced pesticide (such as the synthetic form of pyrethrin, called pyrethroid). Always read and follow all label directions and cautions to the letter, no matter what type of product you are using.

Agricultural Lime
See Lime.

Azadirachtin
Azadirachtin is sold under the trade names Neem, Bioneem, Neem-Away, Rose Defense and others. Toxic to bees. This is a broad-spectrum insecticide

produced from a tropical tree called *Azadirachta indica*. The active ingredient, azadirachtin, works two ways on insects: first, once sprayed on a plant, it keeps many insects from even landing; second, it disrupts the internal workings of a wide variety of pests, usually causing death within a few days. Controls aphids, beetles, caterpillars, locusts, mealybugs, spider mites and whiteflies. Interestingly, recent tests indicate azadirachtin also works as a fungicide, controlling black spot, mildew, rust and other diseases.
Toxicity rating: Caution.

Azadirachtin, the active ingredient derived from the neem tree, kills a wide variety of insect pests, including this grapevine beetle.

Bacillus popilliae

Bacillus popilliae is sold under the trade names Milky Spore, Doom and others. A special strain of bacterium that kills the white grubs of Japanese beetles.
Toxicity rating: Caution.

Bacillus popilliae *works like magic to control the grubs of Japanese beetles. Just read and follow all the label directions carefully and you'll be amazed at the results.*

Bacillus thuringiensis

Bacillus thuringiensis is sold under the trade names Dipel, Thuricide, Javelin and others. Several strains of bacterium including *Bacillus thuringiensis kurstaki, B. t. israeliensis* and *B. t. san diego,* each of which kills a specific pest, including caterpillars, Colorado potato beetles, European corn borer and mosquito larvae. Safe to use around humans, pets, birds and fish. Also available in granules.
Toxicity rating: Caution.

Bt, Btk or Btsd

See *Bacillus thuringiensis.*

Recent tests have shown that a simple mixture of baking soda and water is effective in controlling the disease anthracnose.

Baking Soda

Baking soda is sold simply as baking soda. May be harmful to fish. Recent tests have shown that a simple mixture of common baking soda and water (mixed at the ratio of 4 teaspoons baking soda to 1 gallon water; if possible, $2^{1}/_{2}$ tablespoons of ultrafine horticultural oil added to the mix will help the solution stick to foliage longer) works in preventing anthracnose, black spot and powdery mildew. Repeat spray every two weeks.
Toxicity rating: None.

Bordeaux Mix

See Copper Compounds.

Chitin

Chitin is sold under the trade name Clandosan. It is a soil amendment made up from the substance that forms the exoskeletons of

insects and crustaceans. When incorporated into garden soil, it produces an environment that kills harmful nematodes.
Toxicity rating: Caution.

Chitin, when incorporated into garden soil, produces an environment that kills harmful soil-borne nematodes.

Copper Barriers

Copper barriers are thin strips of copper metal. Slugs and snails won't cross over the copper strips, because the combination of their slime and the copper is thought to produce a mild electrical shock. Great for use around the tops of raised bed gardens, copper strips are available, usually by the roll, in nurseries and garden centers. Some types are backed with an adhesive, making installation easy.

Toxicity rating: None.

Copper Compounds

Copper compounds are sold under the trade names Bordeaux mix (a mixture of copper sulfate and agricultural lime), Kocide 101 and others. Toxic to fish. Copper sulfate is the most basic form and is available in liquid forms, as a wettable powder and as a dust. These are broad-spectrum fungicides and bactericides to prevent brown rot, downy mildew, fireblight, peach leaf curl and shothole diseases.

Toxicity rating: Caution.

Simple and effective: Snails and slugs won't cross a copper strip because their slime on the copper results in a slight electrical shock.

Used by generations of gardeners, copper compounds effectively control many diseases, including downy mildew on corn.

Diatomaceous Earth

Diatomaceous earth is the skeletal remains of single-celled marine algae. The minute, sharp edges of each particle cut into soft-bodied insects, causing death. Agricultural-grade or natural diatomaceous earth are the forms for use in the garden; swimming-pool-grade diatomaceous earth does not have the same insect-killing attributes. Effective against slugs, snails, aphids, mites, earwigs and other soft-bodied pests. May harm honeybees, but harmless to mammals, earthworms and birds. Wear protective gear when applying diatomaceous earth; may cause eye and lung irritation.

Toxicity rating: Caution.

Escar-Go

See Iron Phosphate.

Floating Rowcover

See Rowcover.

If you're diligent with your applications, diatomaceous earth is surprisingly effective in preventing slugs and snails from entering your garden.

A relatively new product, fungicidal soap controls powdery mildew on a wide variety of crops.

Fungicidal Soap

Fungicidal soap is sold under the trade name Soap Shield. This broad-spectrum fungicide is a mixture of fixed copper and potassium salts of fatty acids derived from plants and animals. Controls a wide variety of diseases, including black rot, black spot, botrytis (gray mold), leaf spot and powdery mildew.
Toxicity rating: Caution.

Horticultural Oil

Horticultural oil is sold under the trade names Sun Spray, Volck, Oil-Away and others. Toxic to fish. These products smother insects, and are especially effective against aphids, lacebugs, mealybugs, scale insects, spider mites and whiteflies. There is a lightweight horticultural oil (sometimes called summer, superior or verdant oil) that can be used during the growing season, and a heavier form for use during the dormant season. Do not use the heavier dormant oil spray during the growing season, as it can burn, or even kill, plants.
Toxicity rating: Caution.

Horticultural oil is especially effective against mealybugs.

Insecticidal Soap

Insecticidal soap is sold under the trade names Safer and others. Toxic to fish. Insecticidal soaps are mild poisons extracted from the potassium salts naturally present in the fatty acids found in animals and plants. They are effective on soft-bodied insects like aphids and spider mites, but not on hard-bodied insects like beetles. The salts enter the cell walls of the insects and cause death. To be effective, an insect must actually come into contact with the soap, so fast-flying insects that flee the spray do, in fact, get away free.

The risks from insecticidal soap—to humans, domestic animals and the environment, are very low; and it does not leave a harmful residue on edible plants. Safe to use indoors as well as outside. Some caution must still be taken with its application, however: As effective as it is against harmful soft-bodied insects, insecticidal soap kills soft-bodied beneficial insects, as well.
Toxicity rating: Caution.

Control aphids, an all-too-common pest of many food-producing plants, with insecticidal soap.

Iron Phosphate

Iron phosphate is sold under the trade name Escar-Go. It is the active ingredient in an effective slug and snail killer. Safe for use around pets and wildlife. The iron phosphate breaks down and becomes part of the soil.
Toxicity rating: Caution.

Lime

When gardeners talk about lime, they're not talking about citrus. The lime they are referring to is ground limestone and is very effective in raising the pH of garden soil. Dolomitic limestone is the recommended form, as it adds magnesium as well as calcium to the soil. Follow manufacturer's directions for application rates (which are also affected by soil type and the present pH of the soil).
Toxicity rating: Caution.

Nosema locustae

Nosema locustae is sold under the trade names Nosema, Grasshopper Attack and others. Microscopic protozoa that kill grasshoppers and crickets. Usually sold in bait form.
Toxicity rating: Caution.

Nosema locustae contains microscopic protozoa that kill those voracious pests known as grasshoppers. Proper application is essential; read and follow all label directions carefully.

Rotenone

Extremely toxic to fish, but not toxic to bees. This is one of the most powerful of all natural insecticides. It is derived from several tropical plants and works as a contact poison against many pests, including caterpillars, corn borers, flea beetles, harlequin bugs, leaf-eating beetles, leafhoppers, scale insects, squash bugs, squash vine borers and thrips. Wear a mask when applying; may irritate skin, so wear protective clothing.
Toxicity rating: Caution.

Rotenone is an effective weapon against squash vine borers, killing them on contact.

Rowcovers offer the home gardener simple and successful protection against insect pests.

Rowcovers

Rowcovers are sold under a variety of trade names including Reemay, Agryl, Agrofabric and others. Available in various widths, and normally sold in rolls, rowcovers are lightweight, spunbonded synthetic material. Most types admit 75 to 85 percent of the available sunlight and are solid enough to prevent the entrance of any insect that doesn't emerge from the soil. Because they are so effective, be sure to remove the covers at flowering time on any plants that need pollination to yield well, as rowcovers will even keep bees out. Simply drape the material over the plant or row and pin the edges or weight them to the soil with stones or boards. Any slack in the material should be left in the center, as the fabric is so light that, as the plants grow, they'll lift it with them.
Toxicity rating: None.

Sticky Traps

Sticky traps capitalize on the fact that insects perceive colors differently from humans and seem to mistake the colors white, light blue and yellow for plants and flowers they're attracted to. Most nurseries and garden centers carry pre-made sticky traps: rectangles of plastic or other painted material, with a coating of sticky adhesive. Whiteflies, thrips and aphids appear to be attracted to yellow; some thrips are attracted to light blue, and tarnished plant bugs and flea beetles are attracted to white. Follow manufacturer's directions for placement.
Toxicity rating: None.

Sulfur

Sulfur is sold as Garden Sulfur, the trade name of Safer Garden Fungicide, and others. Longtime preventative treatment for black spot, brown spot, gray mold, powdery mildew, rust and other diseases. Sulfur has also been shown to be effective in controlling aphids, scale insects, thrips, and is especially effective against mites. Available in a variety of forms, including dust, wettable powder and liquid sulfur.
Toxicity rating: Caution.

Aphids are attracted to yellow and will unwittingly fly onto the surface of a yellow-colored sticky trap.

White Sticky Traps
See Sticky Traps.

Yellow Sticky Traps
See Sticky Traps.

Old-fashioned and tried-and-true: Garden sulfur is effective in controlling mites.

SYNTHETIC PESTICIDES AND FUNGICIDES

Synthetic pesticides (what many people refer to as "chemical" pesticides) are largely the product of technology developed during World War II. These products proliferated in the home garden market during the postwar years until research indicated that some had negative, long-term environmental impact. Eventually, some were completely banned by the EPA, or banned for home use. In the descriptions that follow, the words *systemic*, *contact* and *broad-spectrum* are used. Systemic means the product is actually absorbed by the plant, making the plant itself toxic (which means it kills any insect that sucks or chews on the plant). Contact, as in "kills on contact," means the product kills insects when they ingest it or come into contact with it. Broad-spectrum means a product kills a wide range of pests, as opposed to a product that singles out a particular insect or group of insects.

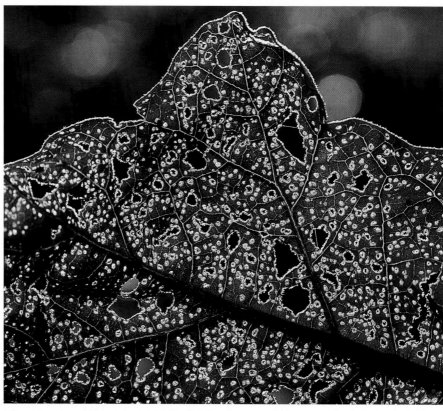

The active ingredient carbaryl kills flea beetles on contact.

Captan is a synthetic fungicide that controls the disease known as leaf spot.

Captan
Captan is toxic to bees and fish and may cause serious eye injury (wear eye protection). Controls brown and black rot and leaf spots.
Toxicity rating: Danger.

Carbaryl
Carbaryl is sold under the trade name Sevin. It is highly toxic to bees and fish. A broad-spectrum insecticide, it kills insects on contact (it is not systemic), including beetles, caterpillars, fleas, spittlebugs, ticks and other pests. Carbaryl also comes in granule form.
Toxicity rating: Caution.

Carbaryl Bait or Granules
See Carbaryl.

Chlorothalonil
Chlorothalonil is sold under the trade name Daconil. Toxic to fish and may cause eye and skin damage (wear protection). A broad-spectrum fungicide that controls black spots, various blights, botrytis (gray mold), leaf spot, powdery mildew and scab.
Toxicity rating: Warning.

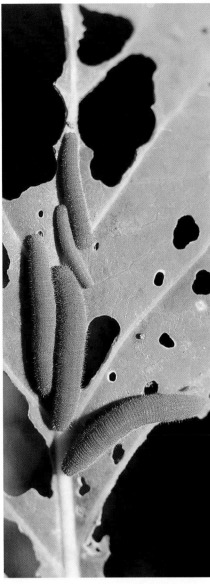

Diazinon can control cabbage butterfly larvae, and caterpillars of all kinds.

Diazinon

Diazinon is highly toxic to fish, bees and birds. A broad-spectrum insecticide that kills pests on contact, including ants, aphids, beetles, caterpillars, fleas, ticks, white grubs and other insects.
Toxicity rating: Caution.

Malathion

Malathion is toxic to bees and fish. A broad-spectrum contact insecticide that kills aphids, caterpillars, lace bugs, mealybugs, thrips and other pests.
Toxicity rating: Warning.

Maneb

Maneb is highly toxic to fish. A broad-spectrum fungicide to control various blights, leaf spot, mildew, rust and other diseases.
Toxicity rating: Caution.

Metaldehyde

Metaldehyde is sold under the name Bug-Geta and Slug-Geta. It is highly toxic to all wildlife (and domestic pets), including birds and fish. A molluscicide that kills slugs and snails.
Toxicity rating: Caution.

Mycobutanil

Mycobutanil is sold under the trade name Immunox. A broad-spectrum, systemic fungicide that controls black spot, mildew, rust and other diseases.
Toxicity rating: Caution.

Pyrethroid

Pyrethroid is the synthetic form of the naturally occurring poison pyrethrin. Toxic to bees. It is sold under a variety of trade names, including Deltamethrin,

The synthetic fungicide maneb controls the disease rust (shown above).

Permethrin, Remethrin, Sumithrin, Tetramethrin and Tralomethrin. May be harmful to fish. It kills aphids, ants, beetles, caterpillars, fleas, houseflies, hornets, leafhoppers, mealybugs, thrips, wasps and whiteflies.
Toxicity rating: Caution.

Synthetic forms of pyrethrum, known as pyrethroids, kill all types of beetles, including Japanese beetles.

BENEFICIAL INSECTS

The idea of using what are commonly called "beneficial insects" to control damaging insects has really caught on in recent years. The following "good guys" are surprisingly effective in controlling a wide variety of garden pests. To keep them in your yard, you'll have to make them feel at home. For one person's experience in creating a favorable environment for beneficial insects, read "A Balanced Approach" on pages 30-35. You may be able to find beneficial insects at your local nursery or garden center; if you have trouble locating what you need, a large number of mail-order sources exist. See page 151 for a list of suppliers.

Aphid Midges

The larva of this tiny black fly eats aphids. In its adult form, it eats the sap, or "honeydew" produced by aphids. Sold as pupae, they should be distributed on the soil or on plants affected with aphids.

Ladybugs

Ladybugs are famous for eating large quantities of aphids, but they'll also eat mites, scale, mealybugs and whiteflies. As flying insects, there's no guarantee they'll stay in your garden, but because they don't fly at night, releasing them in the evening increases the chances they'll stick around—at least for a while. Recommendations vary as to how many ladybugs you'll need in an average-sized garden to be effective—anywhere from one cup to one quart.

Ladybug, ladybug, don't fly away home! Stay in my garden, where you do your good work controlling the bad guys.

For as small as they are and as delicate as they look, green lacewing larvae are surprisingly effective good guys. Encourage lacewing larvae at all costs.

Lacewing Larvae

Lacewing larvae are voracious eaters, consuming large quantities of aphids, caterpillars, leafhoppers, mealybugs, some scales, spider mites, thrips and young whiteflies, over a period of about three weeks. Lacewings are usually sold as eggs and should be placed on plants, approximately four for every square foot of garden.

Beneficial Nematodes

Nematodes are extremely small roundworms, barely large enough to be seen without a magnifying glass. There are basically two species of beneficial nematodes: *Steinernema carpocapsae* (Sc for short) and *Heterohabditis bacteriophora* (Hb for short), along with several strains of each. Each strain works against a specific pest; consult your supplier for proper selection and application rates. They are usually mixed with water and applied directly to garden soil. They are harmless to earthworms, but attack hundreds of soil-borne pests, including the pupae of harmful insects.

Experience suggests that it's best to use only one strain of beneficial nematodes per garden plot, as different strains don't seem to coexist well together.

Predator Mites

Both the adult form of predator mites and their immature nymphs are effective controls against harmful types of mites, including spider mites. There is also a species of predator mite that eats thrips. Usually shipped in the adult stage; be sure to release them in the garden as soon as you receive them.

Parasitoid Wasps

Don't confuse these with yellow jackets or other wasps; parasitoid wasps are so tiny that four of them could fit on the head of a pin, and they don't sting. They do, however, consume large quantities of garden pests, including caterpillars, cutworms and whiteflies. Several species are available, each of which consumes specific pests: consult your supplier to get the right species and for information on releasing these tiny wasps in your garden.

Add the Western predator mite to your list of garden "good guys."

SOLARIZING SOIL

A double layer of clear plastic, held slightly above ground and sealed at the edges, heats the soil beneath in a process called "solarizing." Solarizing is suprisingly effective against a number of soil-borne pests, including nematodes.

Solarizing soil is basically using clear plastic to trap the heat from the sun to raise the temperature of the soil high enough to kill harmful organisms. These include the fungus that causes crown gall and damping off, various wilts and blights, and weed seeds. It's easy and surprisingly effective, and the benefits can last several years. During the hottest part of the year, start by removing all plants and weeds. Till the soil and smooth it out with a rake. Water the area well; it should be damp to a depth of 12 inches. Cover the bed with sheet of clear plastic from 1- to 4-mil thick (black plastic won't "cook" the soil). Add another layer of clear plastic, with spacers between the two (spacers can be anything from bricks to empty soda cans laid on their sides. Cover the edges of the plastic with soil. Keep the plastic clean of dirt and debris; leave it in place for 4 to 8 weeks—the longer the better.

SOURCE LIST

The first place to look for garden supplies and pest control products is your local nursery or garden center. Recent years have seen dramatic improvements in the local availability of not just the standard products, but of alternatives ones, as well. If you have trouble finding what you need locally, the following mail-order supply companies offer excellent selections of pest and disease control products. All information was accurate as of press time.

Arbico
Box 4247 CRB
Tucson, AZ 85738
800/827-2847
www.arbico.com
arbico@aol.com
catalog: no charge

The Beneficial Insect Company
244 Forrest Street
Fort Mill, SC 20715-2325
803/547-2301
www.bugfarm.com

Biofac
P.O. Box 87
Mathis, TX 78368
800/233-4914

Bio Ag Supply
710 South Columbia
Plainview, TX 79072
800/746-9900
wwinters@texasonline.net
catalog: no charge

Bountiful Gardens
18001 Shafer Ranch Road
Willits, CA 95490
707/459-6410

Bozeman Bio-Tech
1612 Gold Avenue
Bozeman, MT 59715
800/289-6656
www.planetnatural.com
catalog: no charge

The Bug Store
113 West Argonne
St. Louis, MO 63122
800/455-2847
www.bugstore.com
catalog: no charge

Eden Organic Nursery Services
P.O. Box 4604
Hallandale, FL 33008
954/455-0229
www.conseed.com
catalog: no charge

Gardener's Supply Company
128 Intervale Road
Burlington, VT 05401
800/444-6417
www.gardeners.com
catalog: no charge

Gardens Alive!
5100 Schenley Place
Lawrenceburg, IN 47025
812/537-8650
gardener@gardens-alive.com
catalog: no charge

Harmony Farm Supply & Nursery
P.O. Box 460
Graton, CA 95444
707/823-9125
www.harmonyfarm.com
catalog: no charge at bulk mailing, otherwise $2.00.

Home Harvest Garden Supply
3712 Eastern Avenue
Baltimore, MD 21224
800/348-4769
www.homeharvest.com

Integrated Fertility Management
333 Ohme Gardens Road
Wenatchee, WA 98801
800/332-3179

Natural Gardening Company
217 San Anselmo Avenue
San Anselmo, CA 94960
415/456-5060
www.naturalgardening.com

Nature's Control
P.O. Box 35
Medford, OR 97501
541/899-8318
bugsnc@teleport.com
catalog: no charge

Nitron Industries, Inc.
P.O. Box 1447
Fayetteville, AR 72702
800/835-0123
www.nitron.com
catalog: no charge

Peaceful Valley Farm Supply
P.O. Box 2209
Grass Valley, CA 95945
530/272-4769
www.groworganic.com
catalog: free once-a-year mailing, otherwise $2.00.

Ringer Corporation
9959 Valley View Road
Eden Prairie, MN 55344
800/654-1047

Rohde's Nursery and Nature Store
1651 Wall Street
Garland, TX 75041
800/864-4445
www.beorganic.com
catalog: posted on Internet only.

Worm's Way
7850 Highway 37 N
Bloomington, IN 47404-9477
800/274-9676
www.wormsway.com
Catalog: no charge

PLANT HARDINESS ZONE MAP

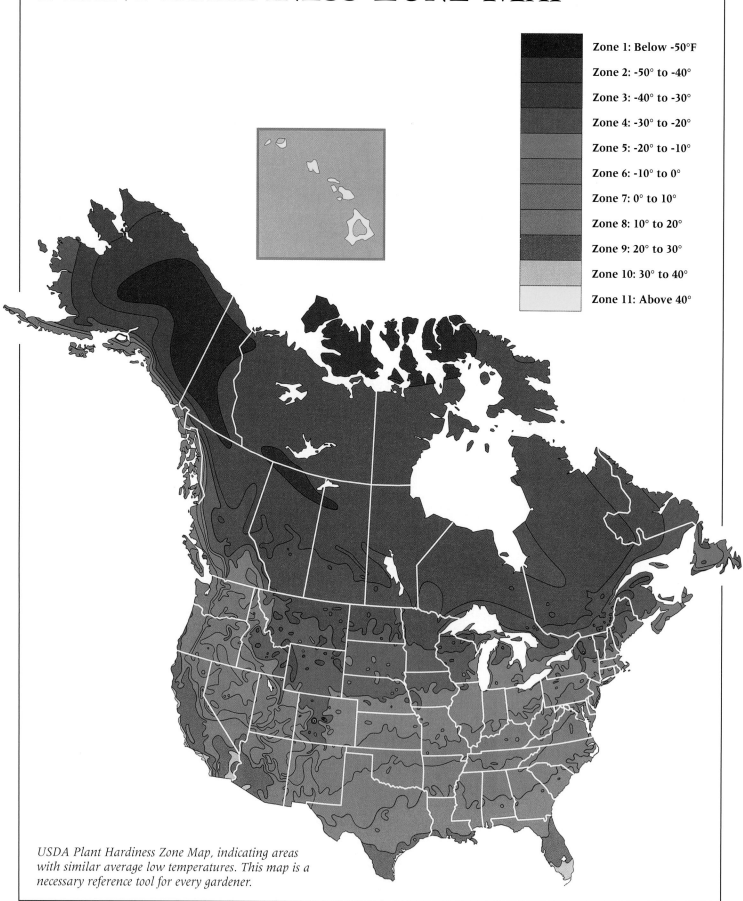

Zone 1: Below -50°F
Zone 2: -50° to -40°
Zone 3: -40° to -30°
Zone 4: -30° to -20°
Zone 5: -20° to -10°
Zone 6: -10° to 0°
Zone 7: 0° to 10°
Zone 8: 10° to 20°
Zone 9: 20° to 30°
Zone 10: 30° to 40°
Zone 11: Above 40°

*USDA Plant Hardiness Zone Map, indicating areas
with similar average low temperatures. This map is a
necessary reference tool for every gardener.*

INDEX OF PLANTS

GENERAL INDEX

PHOTO/ILLUSTRATION CREDITS

PRINCIPAL PHOTOGRAPHY BY DAVID CAVAGNARO

ADDITIONAL PHOTOGRAPHERS

NAOG Garden Archive pp. 20, 79, 84, 85, 101, 112, 117, 140, 141; **Bill Marchel** pp. 22, 24, 25, 26 both; **Animals, Animals:** ©**Ted Levin** p. 23; ©**Leach, OSF** p. 27; ©**Richard Shiell** p. 28; ©**Robert Maier** p. 29; ©**Nigel J. Smith** pp. 139, 142; ©**Tom Edwards** p. 141; ©**Jack Clark** pp. 141, 143, 145, 149; ©**Gerard Lacz** p. 142; ©**Bill Beatty** p. 142; **Rosalind Creasy** pp. 30, 31 both, 32 all, 33 both, 34 both, 35 both, 114, 115, 124, 125, 138, 139; **Robert Creasy** p. 30; **Earth Scenes:** ©**Phil Degginger** pp. 79, 143, 146; ©**J. McCammon, OSF** p. 79; ©**Maximillian Stock Ltd.** p. 93; ©**Richard Kolar** p. 131; ©**Steven Needham/Envision** pp. 91, 117, 131; **Bill Johnson** pp. 140, 143, 144, 145, 147(2), 148, 149

ILLUSTRATORS

Eric Bjorlin/RKB Studios pp. 11, 12 both, 13, 14, 16, 17, 23, 24, 27, 28; **Bryan Liedahl** pp. 38 both, 40 all, 42, 43 both, 44, 45, 47, 48, 49, 52 both, 53, 54, 55, 56, 57 both, 59 both, 60(2); **George Ostroushko** pp. 39 both, 41, 42, 43 both, 44, 45, 47, 48, 49, 52 both, 53, 54, 55, 57, 58 both, 60, 61 both; **Jim Sansovich/RKB Studios** pp. 41, 46 both, 47, 50 both, 51(2), 53(2), 55, 56; **Bill Reynolds** pp. 44, 150